THE NIGHT BEFORE CHRISTMAS

Also by Alice Taylor

Memoirs
To School Through the Fields
Quench the Lamp
The Village
Country Days
The Parish

Poetry
The Way We Are
Close to the Earth
Going to the Well

Fiction
The Woman of the House
Across the River
House of Memories

Essays
A Country Miscellany

Diary
An Irish Country Diary

Children's
The Secrets of the Oak

ALICE TAYLOR

The Night Before Christmas

BRANDON

A Brandon Paperback

This edition published in 2008 by Brandon
an imprint of Mount Eagle Publications
Dingle, Co. Kerry, Ireland, and
Unit 3, Olympia Trading Estate, Coburg Road, London N22 6TZ, England

Copyright © Alice Taylor 1994

The author has asserted her moral rights

ISBN 9780863223921

2 4 6 8 10 9 7 5 3 1

Cover design: Anú Design
Typesetting by Red Barn Publishing, Skeagh, Skibbereen
Printed in the UK

To Sean for my stone steps

Contents

Christmas Past

NED LIFTED THE latch on the door into Christmas when the muscatel raisins appeared on his counter. They were big, soft and juicy and arrived with the ordinary raisins, sultanas and currants in mid-November. Ned weighed them all into stiff brown paper bags and tied them with cord that he kept on the counter in a tin box. The cord snaked its way out through a hole at the top of the can and Ned had the knack of winding it around his fingers and cracking it effortlessly.

He calculated exactly how many pounds of fruit he would sell as his customers' ways and practices were well known to him. He knew that Mrs Casey made three cakes, one for her sister in England, another for her own family and a third one that "himself" would have eaten before the festive season was quite upon her. Then there was Martin's mother who had sisters married all over the parish and made a cake for each one of them. Martin, who worked with us, was loud in praise of his mother's baking. She needed a good supply and Ned was not going to see her short. Then there was old Nell who lived alone beside us and wanted everything halved down into little bags; she did not bother to make a cake at all but ate the fruit straight out of the bag by the fire at night, and sometimes I helped her. Ned worked out all his customers' Christmas needs and because fruit was scarce he stored it away into cardboard boxes, and the candied peel was weighed and put into the boxes as well.

When they came to buy their cards, he went through the selection with them. He had red robins for Mrs Casey, who liked her cards to be full of festive cheer, and other ones with long verses for my mother, because she was very particular about the verses in her cards. He consulted and deliberated with them and sometimes consoled them about the loss of a relative in foreign parts who that year no longer had an earthly address.

Every customer got a present. It was a token of appreciation of their patronage throughout the year. Big round barm bracks and seed loaves were all sorted out and allocated to the different homes. He even gave presents to people who owed him money, because those were the days of little red notebooks and people did not always pay on the dot. But Ned was kind-hearted and maybe their grandmother had been a customer in her day; perhaps this generation was not as good to manage, so they needed a bit of help; another family might be going through a bad patch, and anyway Christmas was no time to be thinking of thrifty details.

Of all the Christmas supplies the candles were the last to arrive: big two-pound red and white candles, and he always remembered which customer went for the white and which favoured the red. My mother was a white-candle woman and Mrs Casey favoured the red ones. Every house took three candles: one for Christmas Eve, one for New Year's Eve and one for Little Christmas Eve; but Nell took one for the three nights and sometimes produced it the following year again. Boxes of messages left the shop with the big candles standing in the middle like shepherds' staffs heralding the coming of Christmas.

Though the smell of Ned's shop on that Sunday morning when the muscatel raisins appeared rang the first bell of Christmas in our minds, there were other signs at home around the farm where the whole work pattern was winding down for the season of rest. On the ditches around the fields, the trees were bare and had gone to sleep for the winter. The fields themselves were in turn wet and squelching with rain or hard and barren with frost and snow and they no longer offered sustenance to the animals, who abandoned them for the comfort of the farmyard. We, too, withdrew from the cold world outside and spent our time in the hay-barn playing imaginary games, or around the fire in the kitchen listening to our old friend Bill telling stories, or sometimes being visited by Nell if she wanted something.

My father's work for the year was done, so he had more time to sit by the fire and smoke his pipe, and the game that he sometimes played with us then was "Cat-out-of-that", though he ran it off as "Catouthat." It was a very simple game but it was great fun. You put your hand on his knee, which was crossed over his other leg. Then he rubbed your hand gently, saying "poor pussy" and laid his hand on yours. Then it was your turn to go "poor pussy" on top of his hand with your other hand, and then he came again with his second hand and this interchanging of hands continued and you were lulled into a sense of soothed relaxation. I loved the warm, firm feel of my father's hands, which were well-formed with long, tapering fingers. Then suddenly his hand came down hard and fast on yours and he declared "Catouthat!" The trick was to anticipate the "catouthat" and whip your hand away in time before he landed; then you were the one doing "poor pussy". In our family that game was never forgotten and if in later years somebody was pussy-footing around when more decisive action was required, the comment was passed that it was time for "Catouthat".

It was my mother who calmed things down when the excitement of Christmas got us all worked up, and she poured oil on troubled waters if any of us children had a row, but she never took sides, always telling us that it took two to make a fight. With five sisters close on each other's heels, there was sometimes a free-for-all. But these conflicts never lasted long, and Dan – who always came for Christmas – advised my mother when a row was in progress and rejected appeals that she should act as adjudicator.

"Keep out of it, Missus," he would say; "it's only a fool would come between them."

My brother Tim, who was the eldest, never got caught up in his sisters' arguments and in many ways was like my mother, who believed in peace and quiet. Frances, who was small and dark and just into her teens, was the sister in charge and she organised the rest of us to do the jobs around the kitchen and farmyard. She did it by means of coaxing and blackmail and was very good at labour relations, using the inducement of a long story at bedtime as an enticement to get through undesirable jobs. Teamed with Frances on the board of management was Terry, who was slim and fast-thinking and who would have ten jobs done while I would be looking at them. They were the pair at the top of the family ladder and Phil and I were at bottom with Eileen, who was tall and green-eyed, in between. Phil was quiet, dark and thoughtful, with long thick hair flowing down over her shoulders or coiled around her head. I was the direct opposite to her as I was long-legged, thin and cheeky.

We loved Christmas and threw ourselves whole-heartedly into all the preparations which my mother left in our hands, and maybe we enjoyed Christmas all the better when we had put such effort into all the work leading up to it.

Our diet at the time consisted of home-produced milk, free-range eggs, bacon and home-grown vegetables: wholesome fare but repetitive, and so the thought of the variety that Christmas would bring filled us with great anticipation. Lemonade, sweet cake and chocolates in our home at that time were like manna in the desert.

The changes that Christmas brought made it stand out in our lives like roses in snow. As well as that, the thought of Santa actually coming across the sky to our home filled us with delight, and it was the only occasion when toys or games came into our house. It was a time of great expectations which climaxed with Christmas Eve and Christmas Day, and then the Wren Day brought a burst of colour and music into the quiet countryside. Between Christmas and Little Christmas and for a time afterwards, we wound down slowly in what was the rest period of the farming year. The farm workers took their holidays until the first of February, so they were free then to call on the neighbours and many house-dances were held. But the biggest dance of all was the Oregonman's ball, when all those home from America came together to celebrate their return and to meet the neighbours. It was a time when old friends met and everybody home for Christmas called around to all the houses in the locality. So Christmas was in many different ways the highlight of our year.

The plucking of the geese about eight days before Christmas Day was the first step. Then for the twelve days of Christmas itself we withdrew into the house like squirrels as the work of the farm was put on hold.

So this is the story of work and celebration: the story of a Christmas past that glowed like a warm fire in the middle of a long, cold winter, when the snow covered the ground for many weeks and I was nine years old.

Goosey Goosey Gander

THEY WERE A strange couple. He was long-legged and his thin, scrawny neck was thrust forward in a continuous genuflecting movement. Sometimes his head tilted so far in advance that it seemed he might loose his balance and fall forward, but his head always came up in the nick of time and brought him upright again. She was soft and voluptuous, her large white bosom quivering out ahead of her. But there was no question of her losing her balance, for her broad, generous bottom wobbled along behind holding the balance of power.

Every morning they led the other geese down the hilly field at the front of the house on their way to the river. He strode slightly ahead of her, not out of any sense of superiority or lack of courtesy, but simply checking the way forward to make sure that the path was smooth for her, whose richly endowed body barely moved clear of the ground. He was a caring custodian whose restrained protective behaviour cushioned her from the rough patches of their life together.

The only occasion on which he threw caution to the winds was in the mating season when, overcome by a flurry of strong sexual urges, he demanded his copulation rights with excited cries and a flapping of wings. She granted his wishes with queenly tolerance. But when she decided that she had satisfied his needs she rose and tossed him to the ground with a disdainful gesture. It was the only time that she was totally in

control and the gander lost his male composure. He looked as if the occasion had unbalanced him, because instead of his head dipping forward in its usual manner it then went from side to side as if he was caught in a cross-wind. But the goose stood there emitting soothing quacks. She seemed to be telling him: "You'll be all right in a few minutes. Just pull yourself together now, old boy." And the gander did just that. The experience had knocked him sideways, but gradually his head returned to its genuflecting motion and his feathers smoothed down. When he deemed himself to be back in control, he proceeded forward and led his partner in passion down the hilly field to the river, the lesser members of his harem following behind. There he cooled his abating ardour in the soothing waters beneath the trees.

On that bright spring morning, though culinary niceties were not high on his list of priorities, our gander had taken the first step towards providing us with roast goose for our Christmas dinner.

Some weeks later the mother goose herself took the next step when, prompted by natural instinct, she made her nest in a shady corner under the sloping galvanised iron roof of the old stone goose-house. She gathered together bits of hay which she darned into a round, cosy shape with soft down and feathers eased from her ample folds. Then she hunkered in and tested it for size and comfort, but it was not to her satisfaction, so out she waddled again and began a remake. It took her a long time to weave the nest perfectly and during all that time the gander stood on one leg, looking on and nodding his head in approval.

Once she was happy with the state of affairs she sat herself down and laid her first large white egg. It was so enormous compared to the hen eggs that I was fascinated by the size of it. Soon afterwards the other geese followed her example, and as the eggs increased in number my mother stored them in a large dish in the room below the kitchen. They were too large for normal human consumption, though we had one neighbour, an enormous man, who liked one for his breakfast. When the goose had reached her laying quota the hatching instinct took over and she refurbished her brood chamber to a higher level of comfort and was transferred to a safer house. My mother placed the eggs back in the nest, and the goose fluffed herself down on top of them. It was a source of surprise to me that she succeeded in easing her large webbed feet in between the eggs without damaging them. She was soon joined in the hatching chamber by her sister geese and they sat on the eggs for a month, leaving them only to eat and drink, and all the time the faithful gander stood in attendance. Not only was he going to be present at the birth but he supervised every step of the hatching period with paternal care.

The day the first gosling tapped his tentative head through the soft embryonic curtain behind the crumbling white shell was a day of great excitement, and as the remaining eggs cracked open, the nests turned from a pool of milk-white shells into a sea of butter-yellow goslings. My mother assisted in the removal of the discarded shells, a feat which required perfect timing and cool courage because the parties involved did not welcome gynaecological intervention and could quite readily bite the helping hand. On the morning when the proud mothers paraded their bright-yellow little ones out of their house the gander danced with joy and led them down to the water. He was a wonderful father, prepared to take on any threat to his family, whom he protected with outstretched flapping wings and hissing beak. When he went into attack in full battledress he was a formidable assailant and the other farm animals who might have considered a soft gosling a dainty dish quickly changed their minds after an encounter with the doting daddy. As his fluffy brood grew into leggy teenagers he kept them in line as well. During the long summer days they roamed the fields and came home at night to their smelly goose-house. They seemed to have no objection to the pungent conditions, because when my father cleaned it out and gave them fresh bedding, they quickly reduced it to its former state.

They passed an idyllic summer grazing the fields and swimming in the river. The only thing to challenge their carefree existence was the wily fox who roamed around the farmyard at night looking for unlocked doors, and every night we had to ensure that their house was made secure against him. Perhaps the high point of their year came on the evening of the threshing when, once the thresher had pulled out of the haggard, they descended on the spilt grain and the mounds of chaff with screeching anticipation and began a glorious feast which lasted for a few days, during which time they kept up a continual chorus of cackling appreciation. Then they went out on to the stubble fields where the grain had come from and here they continued a meticulous search for the last of the left-overs.

Come November the goslings were long-legged, fit young geese which my mother called grass geese, but they were in no condition to provide the wherewithal for a succulent Christmas dinner, a situation that had to be remedied. It was time, my mother declared, to fatten them up. They were put into the goose-house where they gobbled up buckets of sloppy mash; they grew fat and inactive and loved all the attention. My brother used to look in at them, shaking his head at the unfairness of it all, and quote a few lines from a poem that he liked:

Alas, regardless of their doom,
The little victims play;
No fears have they of ills to come
Or cares beyond today.

Then one day the jennet was tackled to the crib, which was created by putting railings around the creamery cart, and it was filled with fat, screeching geese. They were now on their way to the Christmas market. But the best of them, seven in all, were held back for home cooking and to provide Christmas gifts for town relatives. We would need three ourselves: one for Christmas Day, one for New Year's Day and one for Little Christmas, or the Women's Christmas as my father called it. The other four were for aunts and cousins. Mother goose and the gander did not seem to notice that their family was shrinking. About ten days

before Christmas they were left totally childless when
my mother declared that "plucking the geese" night
was upon us. For a few days previously the poor geese
had been starved, and as soon as we came home from
school that evening we had to sit down at the kitchen
table and get the lessons out of the way. This meant
that we did not have the help of our old friend Bill who
lived on top of the hill behind our house and who came
every night to help us with our lessons, but even our
loyal and trusted Bill was going to abondon ship that
night. The early lessons session was my mother's plan
for clearing the decks for the marathon night of plucking; we were the only work-force available and as we
were a reluctant brigade she was eliminating potential
excuses.

The duty of executioner fell upon my mother simply
because no one else would be party to it. Early in their
goose lives my father had declared to her that they
were "your geese", which applied especially if they got
into the meadows where they flattened the uncut hay
and left evidence of their lack of toilet training.

We hated the plucking of the geese, the only redeem-
ing feature of which was that it meant that Christmas
was around the corner. The actual killing was a bar-
baric ritual and when the corpses emerged from the
death chamber, which was the room below the kitchen
on the night, each had a bloody slit across the back of
its head. They were still warm and frightened the wits
out of me when they gave an occasional shudder as
their life blood ebbed away into a jam pot.

When they were all belly-up on the kitchen table with
their necks dangling above the floor, my mother organised her plucking team. It was desirable that they
should be plucked straight away as a warm goose was
easier to pluck than a cold one. A big box was placed in

the centre of the kitchen and we were all ranged
around it as if we were conducting a seance. Each child
had a goose and the strict instruction was not to tear
the skin as this blemished the table presentation of the
goose. Sometimes the feathers came freely, but invari-
ably at some stage you hit a trouble spot when you felt
that the poor goose was trying to hold on to its cover
and protect its modesty. But my mother was intent on
baring all, so each one of us stuck with our goose until
we arrived at the soft downy feathers that wafted up
our noses, causing us to sneeze and blow feathers in all
directions. The pen feathers were the worst of all and
slowly and laboriously had to be eased out one by one.
My mother finished first and ended up with a smooth
white goose as clean as a whistle with not a tear in
sight. But from then on it was downhill all the way
until the final goose, which had changed pluckers many
times, ended up looking as if a third-rate plastic sur-
geon had done a rush job on her. Finally, when they had
all been parted from their feathers, my mother tied
their webbed legs together with yellow binder twine
and we all joined in chanting:

Christmas is coming,
The geese are getting fat,
Please put a penny
In the old man's hat.
If you haven't got a penny
A halfpenny will do
And if you haven't got a halfpenny
Then God bless you.

When the last goose had had her legs tied, the sorting
out of the feathers started. My mother had different
boxes for different grades of feathers, and while we had
been directed to the right box during plucking, there
had been quite a few mix-ups which she now sorted out.

Then the different boxes had to be carried to the attic at the top of the house and here they would stay until the filling for pillows, cushions or feather ticks was required.

The next job was to transport the geese to the old stone house at the end of the garden, which was known as the turf-house, though I never remember it holding turf. That morning the ivy-covered house had been scrubbed out in preparation for its duty as a funeral parlour. Earlier that year it had been the goslings' delivery chamber when they had chipped their way out of the big goose eggs into the light of day. Now we made our way there, each of us bearing a naked goose aloft, our way lighted by the combined power of the moon and my father's storm lantern that he used for checking the cows in their stalls at night. When we arrived into the low house, the moonlight deserted us and the storm lantern sent scary shadows up and down the old stone walls. We handed them one by one to my mother and she hung them off the rafters, where they swung with outstretched wings and heads pointed downwards like fallen angels.

Out in the goose-house the mother goose and the gander cuddled up close together. Their year's work was done and the gander was looking forward to the spring.

Getting the Holidays

A LL THAT WEDNESDAY we waited for him to make the announcement, but as the shadows of the grey winter's evening crept in and obliterated the long sooty cobwebs hanging from the rafters, our hearts sank sadly into our wet muddy boots and we became rows of grey lumps of misery slumped along the desks in front of the Master. He had it in his power to ignite us into airborne balloons of joy with a declaration of intent that we were to get the holidays on Friday. We knew that we just had to get them on Friday as Christmas was the following week and we never went to school on Christmas week. But until the official announcement was made there was a sense of uncertainty about the whole thing. The Master controlled everything in our school world and we thought that maybe if he so decided he could postpone Christmas. Our heads told us that he could not, but our hearts did not feel so sure. All we wanted for the floodgates of our expectations to be opened was to hear the magic words "Christmas holidays". He was the angel who could declare unto us that Christmas was about to begin but for some reason best known to himself he remained silent while dozens of pleading eyes implored him to relent. That day he choose to keep the good news to himself.

I watched him from the back seat of the draughty classroom. He stood on the high rostrum at the top left-hand corner of the square room from where he had a grandstand view of any dubious activities that might

take place. His glasses, which normally resided on top of his iron-grey hair, were now perched on his long nose as he corrected our copy-books. They seemed to be bringing him little pleasure as occasionally he peered in disapproval at us out over the top of his glasses. He was strict but fair and usually we liked him well enough, but his silence now meant that he was not our favourite person. Suddenly he stepped down off the rostrum and walked along between the desks, rattling the change in his pocket. I was very impressed by the fact that he had enough money to make such a jingle and I sometimes tried to estimate how much money exactly he had in the pocket of his shiny brown pants. He was the only man in my everyday world who had soft white hands and polished shoes, and I wondered what it would be like to live in a world of polished shoes.

As the Master turned his back to walk up the room I

caught my sister Eileen's eye across the desks. Normally we were good friends but today a cold war was being waged between us. The previous morning I had sneaked a new cardigan to school under my coat. It was a bright red and yellow Fair Isle and I loved it especially because it was my first new, shop-bought cardigan. Most of our clothes were home-made or hand-me-downs, so this bright cardigan with its soft feel was very special. It was for Sunday wear only but I wanted to show it off to my tormentor Maura; she was the only girl in the class who did not believe in Santa, which made her enemy number one in my world. I had boasted about it to her and she had challenged me to wear it to school or otherwise she would not believe that I actually had it. So after breakfast I had doubled back upstairs and put it on under my coat. In doing this I knew that I had broken one of my mother's rules, but I felt it was worth it to see the look of surprise on Maura's face. That evening my sister cornered me coming home from school.

"Why did you wear your Sunday cardigan?" she asked.

"No why," I told her.

"I know why," she countered.

"You don't," I told her.

"Oh yes I do," she asserted.

"Why so?" I challenged.

"You wanted to impress Butter-Belly Bill."

"I did not!" I screamed at her.

"You did so," she declared. "I saw him picking up your pencil off the ground when it rolled off the end of your desk."

"Shut up!" I shouted at her. "I don't even like Billy Tobin and I think that you're a horrible snot to call him that name just because he's fat." And I ran down the field ahead of her calling back over my shoulder: "Nellie, Nellie. Nellie with the Timber Belly!" That evened the score but we still were not "good friends". Now, behind the Master's back, I hung off the end of the desk and stuck my tongue out at her as far as was physically possible. In return she put her two thumbs into the corner of her mouth and extended it to the edges of her face and screwed up her eyes until they disappeared into two narrow slits.

The Master did a fast turn on one heel, bringing a temporary cease-fire to our facial warfare. Then he walked over to the big old fireplace in the corner. The only thing our school fire heated was the chimney, but it coughed out smoke that covered the map on the wall overhead with black soot so that when we were being taught Irish geography, it was first necessary to give the Galtee Mountains a swipe of a feather duster to unveil their geographic dimensions. The Master peered up at the school clock and then he clapped his hands together and said in a loud voice: *"Amach libh."* *

This announcement stimulated a stampede for the door which resulted in a body jam in the porch where straining hands pulled assorted coats from the rusty hooks overhead. Then we tore out the door, dragging coats and sacks on over our shoulders, and sloshed out through the sodden schoolyard, heads down, intent only on reaching the comfort of home to ease off damp boots and thaw out frozen toes in front of the fire. Due to the cold and to the disappointment of no holiday announcement, we were in no humour to prolong the journey

My father met us in the yard where he was bringing straw to the stables. "How are the scholars?" was his usual salute when he met us coming home from school and this evening, having viewed our faces, he also queried: "No news of the holidays?"

* Out you go

"No," was the dismal confirmation.

"Maybe he'll forget to give them to ye," he grinned, rubbing salt into the wound.

When we reached the kitchen my mother was far more comforting. "Tomorrow without a doubt," she told us, "and the only reason that he did not tell ye today was because ye would not do another stroke of work for him once the excitement of the holidays hit ye."

What she said made sense and we all felt better. She had the happy knack of putting everything into perspective, and later that evening when I went out to collect the eggs, I crossed off another day on my series of strokes along the inside of the galvanised door of the hen-house. When the count-down to the Christmas holidays had begun I had got a soft white stone and marked out a series of lines to represent the remaining school days. Every evening it gave me intense pleasure to put a stroke through another day: a step nearer to freedom and to Christmas. Now there were only two strokes left. Tomorrow he would just have to tell us! That night we did our lessons grudgingly and complained that it was "not fair", to which complaint my father had his constant answer that the sooner we learnt that life was not fair the better for ourselves. We were in no humour to listen to his philosophical observations and I wondered if he was like Maura and had never believed in Santy.

The following evening, just before he clapped his hands for the final dismissal, the Master made the long-awaited announcement, which was received with hoots of delight.

That Friday morning we went to school on winged feet. We were getting the holidays! The weather had changed overnight and our muddy gaps were now rock-solid frozen ridges interspersed with pools of black ice. Where the day before we had had to pick our steps to avoid being submerged in mud, now we were free to dance on top of it. The freedom matched our mood, and when we arrived into the hilly field behind the school, we crouched down on our heels and, wrapping our hands around our knees, we sped down the icy path that yesterday had been a mucky stream. One after the other we sped down the icy slope and with every skate the slope became more slippery.

We arrived in school red-nosed and puffing, and though the Master tried to pretend that it was a normal school day, he gave up the struggle at lunchtime and studies gave way to riddles and stories. Then we started to tidy things away. All the copy-books had to be stored in the top of the high press where they would be safe from the rats who took over when we went home. They occupied the world under the floorboards and sometimes did not even wait for us to retreat before they made their appearance. We had to make everything secure against them as they would have a full uninterrupted two weeks in which to call the place their own. The boys went outside to tidy the turf in the shed behind the school and we brought down the cobwebs that were within reach; for the first time since the fire had been lit in the autumn we got to see a clean face on the entire map of Ireland. Maura and I worked together emptying the ink wells and our former struggle for one-upmanship was temporarily put on hold. As the Master locked up the big roll-books in the rostrum and hung the duster over the clean blackboard, we could hear the high and low infants in the room next door banging their small blackboards and ball-frames into their *cófra*.*

The porch where we stored our coats and lunches had to be cleared out of left-overs that had accumulated

* cupboard

since the summer holidays.

"You didn't leave your posh cardigan," my sister whispered to me.

"Shut up!" I shot back, but it was the last round in a dying battle.

The old stone trough that held our lunches had a collection of green-lined milk bottles that had to be collected and distributed to reluctant owners. Nobody recognised their own bottle but everybody recognised their neighbour's and in this way they were all disposed of eventually. We pulled on our coat with smiles on our faces. When the Master turned the big key in the old battered door, it had an air of finality about it. We were free! The school was locked and the blight of doing our lessons no longer hung over us. We breathed sighs of relief. We had the holidays now and were free to get ready for Christmas!

The Christmas Chimney

THE DAY WE saw his camp by the bridge at the bottom of the hill, we knew that Black Ned had arrived to clean our chimney for Santa. Most travelling people moved around the countryside in groups or as part of one large family, but Ned was different. He was a silent loner who came and went quietly.

He never initiated a conversation and barely replied to any questions that were put to him. Once when I asked if he was ever lonely, he looked at me in surprise and said: "No", and then added, which was unusual for Ned, "I like being alone."

A travelling chimney sweep, well over six foot tall, he was almost as thin as one of his own chimney sticks. His clothes were black and greasy and fitted him so tightly that his arms and legs were like narrow branches attached to a tall, slim tree, and when I looked up at him from my nine-year-old height, I thought that Ned went up for ever.

He had a piebald pony and a brightly painted cart under which he sheltered his grey canvas tent. Inside in it lay his long black chimney brushes, and his brown and white wire-haired terrier guarded its entrance with a sharp vicious bark and the hair standing up on the back of his neck. The pony and the terrier were almost the same colour, and while the terrier barked and growled, the pony kicked and would bite if you were foolish enough to come too close. Ned's third travelling

companion was a bantam cock which perched on top of the upheeled cart and crowed shrilly. They were a colourful collection and of them all Ned was the one who made the least noise. To me he was the black spirit of Christmas come to prepare the way for Santa, and I loved to watch him boil his black kettle over the fire outside his tent. He could catch rabbits and pheasants, so he dined well, and the people were generous to him because it was an accepted fact in the neighbourhood that Ned was a gentleman.

On the day of his arrival the kitchen fire was quenched after the breakfast. It was strange to see that corner of the kitchen without the life of the fire. Then the whole recess was cleared of pots and pans. The crane that swivelled back and forth was now bare of its kettles and hangers and its iron leg was lifted out of its underground swivel; the whole clattering menagerie was taken out into the yard and the chimney recess was covered with old coarse bags. Old Minnie, our cat, was evicted from her warm corner under the hob and meowed in protest around the kitchen. It was the one day of the year when the heat of the kitchen fire was missing, and we all felt a little bit like Minnie, that we did not quite know where to put ourselves.

He arrived with a clatter of chimney sticks and no talk and set immediately to work. Ours was a wide chimney and when you stood in under it and looked up you could see the sky, but the amount of sky on view depended on the prevailing soot conditions. To ascertain how things were up along, Ned stooped down to get in under the chimney breast and most of him disappeared up the chimney. He reappeared blacker than before and grunted in characteristically eloquent comment. Ned liked a real dirty chimney and the less of the sky he could see, the louder his grunt of appreciation.

He untied his chimney sticks and, catching the one with the black tarry bristles on top, he pushed it up the chimney and then tied another on to the end of it with a black rag. And so gradually the bundle of sticks on the floor decreased in number and disappeared up the chimney. As the sticks dwindled the soot started to move. It rolled down in billowing clouds and Ned's legs and that corner of the kitchen disappeared in a black fog. It wafted around the rest of the kitchen like black thistledown and slowly covered everything.

It was my job then to run outside and watch for the brush to come out at the top. When its black sooty head emerged triumphant, I shouted in delight and ran to tell Ned's long thin legs that it was after making it to the top. He grunted in satisfaction.

Up and down the chimney, backwards and forwards, he pushed the brushes, adding and subtracting lengths

as the necessity arose. All the time the soot cascaded down in showers. Gradually the showers eased off, then changed to soot flakes and finally dried up completely. Next he got a hoe and scraped down the hidden ledges.

Then I joined Ned to judge the state of the chimney. It was as clean as a whistle and a big patch of blue sky was visible, and so it was ready for Santa. Up along we could even see the iron brads that he could use as footholds on his way down.

When Ned had gone the big return began, but first my sisters took advantage of the opportunity to give that corner of the kitchen a big overhaul. Behind the iron bellows was always a dumping corner for homeless odds and ends, but these were now evicted. Long lost odd stockings saw the light of day for the first time in months, but it was obvious that moths and mice had been on friendly terms with them in the meantime.

When the area behind the bellows had become litter-free, my sister Frances produced the big white goose-wing and whipped out any remaining scraps; dry, grey dust drifted up the chimney. Then the white goose-wing did the rounds of the whole corner, but was no longer so white when it had finished. After that my father decided to oil the bellows, which was a lengthy task because parts of it had to be dismantled, and while this went on we all shivered around the kitchen. Finally it was back in place. The crane was brought in and part of its leg disappeared underground and it swung into position. Then the fire was lit and the pots and kettles returned and we were back in action, but it took the kitchen a good few hours to recover from the freezing it had got.

That night as we sat around the fire Minnie purred in contentment. It had been a rough day for her but now things were back to normal and she was warm again, which was all that mattered in her world. We could smell the newly disturbed soot and a film of it still rested on high, less accessible points around the kitchen. But it was not destined to stay there very long, for Ned's had only been the first step in the Christmas cleaning. Minnie had her only rough day put down, but I knew that I had a few ahead of me when my sisters moved into action around the house in the big Christmas clean-up.

Letter to Santy

IVY TRAILED DOWN over the weather-beaten door, like
tendrils of hair over the face of an old lady. During
its lifetime this door had been pink, green, red and
grey, and then all these colours had faded and peeled
and blended together to give it a soft, multi-coloured,
weather-beaten appearance. In the days after the
plucking of the geese, it became a place of daily pil-
grimage because behind it hid the spirits of Christmas
coming. They hung off the rafters, their yellow legs
bound with brown binder-twine. White, frozen spirits,
they swung with fanned wings and downward beaks,
like swooping angels in the dark shadows of the turf-
house. The peeling boards of the old door had shrunk
with the passage of time, so now I could peer through
the gaps into the eerie gloom inside. Sometimes I
reached upwards and pressed down the rusty latch
and pushed the protesting door, which scraped along
the stone floor. To push the door open completely required more courage than I possessed. I kept the
greater portion of my body safely outside, ready for
flight, in case one of these grey-white ghosts might
spring to life and carry me away on its beak. So I
poked my head in a small opening and peered in awe
at these ashen creatures. They bore little resemblance
now to the plump, white geese which had quacked
comfortably around the straw-filled fattening house
the previous week.

This door was my diary, reserved for recording the

good things of my life. One of the rusty hinges had a
loose nail which I could pull out and with this I
scratched out dates when happy things happened to me
and drew little scenes that held special meaning for me.
Nobody else could make head nor tail of all the scrib-
bling and scratching, but for me they had a secret
meaning. The gaps between the stones around it were
the hiding places for my treasures: coloured sea shells,
odd-shaped stones from the river bed, bits of coloured
glass and an old bird's nest in which I would keep my
letter for Santa until posting time was right.

The night we got the school holidays was set aside for
the major undertaking of writing to Santa. Up until
such time as we saw the Master firmly turn the big iron
key in the gaping old lock we did not feel safe from the
fetters of school to concentrate completely on Christmas;
now, however, it was time to let Santa know that we

were expecting him to call and to advise him as to our requirements.

Our friend Bill from the top of the hill behind our house was the man to take charge of this writing class. After supper that night when we had the ware washed, we gathered around the kitchen table. We covered the table with old copies of the *Cork Examiner* to level the writing surface and to absorb spilt ink. My father decided that it would be a good night to visit the neighbours because writing letters to Santa was not quite his field. Bill directed operations from beside the fire and my mother darned stockings in her usual position under the oil lamp. Because notepaper was a luxury reserved for foreign letters, we had to be satisfied with pages from our school copy-books. My mother placed a bottle of Quink ink in the centre of the table, at least at the point that she considered to be the centre, but that was a debatable point and an argument evolved about what point exactly was the dead centre of the table. A mini tug-of-war with the ink bottle resulted in ink splashes on the *Cork Examiner,* and Bill intervened with the threat that if we did not behave ourselves he would follow in our father's footsteps. We did not really believe him but at the same time were afraid to take the chance. Without Bill, the layout plan and the final decisions on requests and spelling might prove a problem. The final choice of ink-well position was left to him. When he placed it back in the exact spot that my mother had chosen, we all had to be satisfied, but the least satisfied compensated for their disappointment by making faces at those who grinned in victory. In front of each of us was a school copy and the lucky ones had an unused centre page which could be eased out gently from beneath the tin grips.

We were very inexperienced in the art of letter-writing so Bill started us all off with our address at the top right-hand corner. My sister Phil, who loved geography, was not satisfied with the bare address, however, and added Ireland, Europe, and This World. I doubted that Santa needed all those directions, but because she was better at geography than me, I decided to follow suit. The next step was how to address him: Father Christmas, Santa or Santy. We always called him Santy, but then we sometimes called one of the teachers in school Nellie but we would not dare call her that to her face. Was Santy childish and over-familiar? We split on that decision but I stuck to Santy because in my mind I could never think of him as anything other than Santy, and if I called him something else I would think that I was writing to a stranger.

We dipped our "n" pens into the ink. If we went down too deep in the bottle we emerged with a surplus, which resulted in a blob on the copy-book. Sometimes this could be partly absorbed with blotting paper, especially if the blotting paper was white and clean. If the blotting paper did not quite succeed, an ink rubber was brought into action, but over-use of this could result in a hole making its unwelcome appearance. Then you had to start all over again.

It was when we came to the choice of requests that the real problem emerged. We knew exactly what we needed but at the same time we did not want to appear too greedy. This was where Bill debated and advised. I wanted a doll because I had never had one that was entirely my own and I didn't mind how small she was as long as she was mine alone. But I also wanted crayons, a colouring book and a school sack, because my books were always falling out of the sack that I had and it had been patched and sewn up so often that the patches were now being patched. I wondered was I stretching my luck too far to be looking for three things, but Bill advised chancing it, so I listed my needs, satisfied that I had covered everything. When I had my letter written to my satisfaction and laboriously signed, I wrote out an exact copy and hid it in my pocket. My mother produced an airmail envelope, we folded all the letters up neatly and placed them inside, and then my sister Frances addressed it to "Santa, The North Pole". The following day we were waiting for Johnny the Post when he came, and he assured us that it would be on its way that night.

Later that day I went back to the old turf-house door and drew back the ivy. There between the stones was the dried-out bird's nest that was no longer in use because its owner was on her foreign holidays. I eased my letter to Santa out of my pocket and tucked it into the nest. I considered this the ideal resting place because the owner and Santa both belonged to foreign places and came here across the sky. There was the mystery of the unknown about the worlds they both came from; they belonged in the sky and my letter was destined to join them there when the time was right.

On Christmas Eve I would collect my letter from the nest, and as we sat around the fire that night, I would drop it into the blazing sods of turf where it would curl up and join the smoke going up the chimney. My letter to Santa would be recorded in the smoke that went straight up Black Ned's clean chimney and Santa would read my message in the clouds.

Holly Sunday

AFTER MASS WE set out for the wood. Even though our house was surrounded by trees, we had no holly tree and going for the Christmas holly meant a major excursion. It was a cold, wet day, but the weather provided no barrier to our enthusiasm. We dressed ourselves up in what we called our "everyday coats", leaving our Sunday wear hanging in the wardrobe.

We went into the barn where my father usually kept bits of left-over hay-twine which he wound up into little coils and tucked in under the rafters. They were stored high above the block of hay, so we had to climb up the long timber ladder and walk over the spongy hay that bounced up and down under our weight. We found the hidden twine between the swallows' nests, which were hidden behind the barn poles under the rafters, waiting for their summer residents to return from far-away places. Our pockets bulging with hay-twine, we went in pursuit of the next necessity for the success of our undertaking, a saw. This presented a bit of a hurdle to be overcome as my father had a long memory about top-class saws that had gone to the wood and had never again seen the light of day. The easiest approach seemed to be just to take one on the quiet, but he was a step ahead of us and had ensured that there was not a saw in sight. We tried to convince him that his saw would be so safe with us that he would have nothing to worry about, but we finished up with a rusty antique in need of false teeth which, if it had been lost, would not have been missed.

Eventually we set out across the fields, not on the well-worn pathway that was beaten down by our journey to school, but in the opposite direction across strange fields where the ditches were well shrouded in briars, bushes and blackthorn hedges. Some were practically impenetrable with their density of foliage, but even so they were no match for our determination to make a breakthrough. The blackthorn put up the sternest resistance and dug its vicious spikes into our bulky clothes; though we finally broke free the blackthorn wore strips of our coats in victory. We knew nothing about going into reverse to free ourselves from the fetters of briars and branches; in our single mindedness we thought only of going forward. The barbed wire, however, we treated with greater respect: we held it up for each other as we crawled under it on our hands and knees, curving our backs to avoid the barbs. Where it was low we held it down and swung our legs over it, taking care to avoid quivering spikes making contact with long-legged knickers. Sometimes when this happened we struggled free only to find that the tails of our coats had made contact with another spike.

Although the ditches were barriers to be overcome, they were as nothing compared to the river that lay ahead. Normally we crossed this river at a shallow point where it was bridged by large stepping-stones. I usually jumped gingerly from stone to stone, my heart thumping in fright, but I always reached the other bank in a flush of triumph as I jumped from the last stone to land safely on solid ground. But when the river was in flood the stepping-stones disappeared beneath a swirl of foaming brown water.

That day, because it had rained heavily earlier in the

week, the stepping-stones were nowhere to be seen and the river gushed along in an angry torrent. But we had the measure of this river and knew its weakness. At one point it was narrow and when the stepping-stones failed this narrow section provided a second, though less desirable option. Here you could jump across and if you paced yourself well and luck was on your side you could make it dry to the other side. The best jumper went first: we all watched with bated breath as he sailed across and sighed in relief when he landed safely. As the expertise of the jumpers decreased so did the clearing distance at the other side. When my turn came there was no clearing distance at all as I landed in the wet gravel at the edge of the water and had to be hauled out with mud and water oozing out of my high laced-up boots. Once we were all across we cheered in victory and proceeded on our way.

We were glad to reach the wood and shelter from the rain. Inside it was dark and eerie and the trees sighed and dripped on the soft carpet of pine needles and brown and faded leaves that clung to our wet leather boots. No birds sang and it was as if the wood had gone to sleep; we found ourselves whispering until someone asked out loud: "What are we whispering for?" The question broke the sombre silence and we started to shout in order to prove to ourselves that we were not overawed by the dark, cathedral stillness of the wood. We ran around under the trees, hiding behind their trunks and jumping out to frighten each other, and the braver ones forged ahead out of sight where they climbed up into the high branches and swung down like Tarzan letting out bloodcurdling yells. I searched along the path, on the look-out for my special tree that I visited every year. It had a soft mossy trunk with big lumps and hollows and it was easy to imagine that little people lived inside it. At first I could not find it and began to think that it had disappeared when suddenly there it was in front of me, mossier and softer than ever. I ran and put my arms around it but the span was much wider than the length of my arms. Its lowest branches seemed miles above my head, but its trunk was so full of interesting little corners that the temptation to stay and play in them was very strong. Every Christmas I promised myself to make a summer trip but forgot all about it until Holly Sunday again.

Our mission was to gather holly, so eventually we laid our hay-twine along the soft, pine-covered ground in the corner where the holly trees hid amongst taller neighbours. We divided our team into climbers, catchers and wrappers. The climbers had to cut or break off the pieces of holly which in their opinion looked the best, though their judgement was sometimes assisted by their ground crew. My father's saw squeaked and scraped across the branches and proved as useless as we had feared, so the branches were severed by a combination of jolted sawing, cracking and twisting. The catcher was lucky if the branch fell clearly to the ground; sometimes it had to be burrowed out from between other branches while the climber from above shouted instructions and bent the tree in the right direction. The ground crew sorted the collection into different lengths and laid them across the hay-twine. The cream of the crop bore red berries, and as long as we had enough red-berried holly for the Christmas candle and crib we were happy. We had to be careful when tying up the bundles with the hay-twine as the holly did not take too kindly to being tied tightly and scratched and scraped in retaliation.

The next item on the agenda was ivy, and the collection of this was done from the ground. We caught the

tail end of long strips of ivy that were growing up along
the big trees. Sometimes we were lucky and it ran with
us, but sometimes just when we thought we had a fine
length it cracked and we were left holding bare stringy
bits while looking upwards at fine leafy foliage away
above our heads. The ivy was much softer and easier to
handle than the holly, and when we had sufficient we
wound it up into large hoops and tied them together.
Then all that remained for collection was the moss for
the crib and the base of the Christmas tree. Some of the
banks along by the paths had nice moss but the best
bits grew up along the trunks of the old trees. If a tree
was tilted forward the moss seemed to form a coat
along the leaning trunk almost like a saddle on a
horse's back and if you got your fingers neatly in under
it you could lift the large layer off in one go. When this
operation commenced I always tried to lead the moss

gatherers away from my special tree, but someone was
bound to discover it. Then only tears and hysterics on
my part kept his coat on against the winter cold. My
brother lectured me about the need, for the good of the
tree, that it should be relieved of its mossy coat, but I
was not impressed by his argument. All I knew was
that without my coat I felt the cold and I could not see
how it was any different for my special tree. Lectures
on natural conservation cut no ground with me. Finally
my tears won the day and my friend was safe for another year.

With the return of the crows to the wood for the night,
we knew that it was time to go home. They arrived with
a flurry of black wings across the sky and swooped
down with a clatter of squawking that turned the wood
into an echo of demented noise. We came out from
under the trees to find that the rain had stopped and
the freezing early night air hit us across the face like a
cold cloth. Jack Frost was busy laying his grey shroud
across the countryside. The dripping trees of the early
afternoon had been turned into frozen, silent shapes
and the grass crunched beneath our boots.

Burdened with the greenery, our progress was slow
and the bundles had to be shifted regularly as the
thorny holly made a prickly travelling companion.
When we arrived back at the river it was necessary to
get the bundles safely across before we took the jump
ourselves. They had to be thrown over with a good
sense of direction because a miscalculation could result
in a bundle disappearing down the river. Everything
went according to plan, and as I waited to take my running jump, the cold bit my face and numbed my fingers;
my toes in my wet boots felt as if they were outside
rather than inside my thick knitted stockings. It was
luck rather any athletic skill that got me safely back

across the river. As we trudged homewards the moon rose higher in a navy-blue sky and when we stood to look up at the stars I wondered which one of them had come down to light up the crib on that first Christmas night.

When we arrived home we took our holly to the old stone house at the end of the yard where my mother's plucked geese were hanging off the rafters. Here we sorted out our collection into different lots, because tomorrow we would take a bundle each to my grandmother and to Nell and Bill who had no children to go to the wood to collect holly for them.

Nell's Clean Sweep

THE FOLLOWING MORNING I set out for Nell's house with her Christmas holly bundle on my back.

As I left the yard my father called after me: "Will you tell that wan to get Black Ned to clean her chimney while he is around or she'll be burnt to a cinder under that thatch of hers."

"I'll tell her," I shouted back at him, "but she won't do it anyway."

"No," he agreed, "she'll wait until she's in a blaze and then expect foola here to put it out with a big spit."

Nell was a constant source of irritation to my father and he often compared her to her own donkey. He declared that you could neither lead nor drive the pair of them. I had a limited amount of sympathy for his point of view but most of my sympathy was reserved for Nell. She did only what she deemed to be absolutely necessary in the way of household maintenance. The way Nell explained it to me it made great sense. Black Ned would have to be paid, and though he charged very little still Nell did not want to pay up. As well as that, she hated having anybody in around her house. She liked to have the place to herself and I liked it that way as well. I could disappear across the fields to her house and be my own boss there because Nell did not conform to any rules and did not expect me to do so either.

She lived alone in an old thatched house and her only companions were her dog Shep and a collection of cats. She managed her small farm herself, milking her few cows and her goat morning and evening; the neighbours who helped her with the harvest got no thanks and even encountered a great reluctance on Nell's part to feed them on the day. She told them that it was their duty as Christians to help out a neighbour who had no husband to do the heavy work for her. My father would roll his eyes to heaven and tell her that there was not a man born who could put up with her and she would in return assure him that apart from doing the dirty work she had no need for men in her life.

Nell had her own way of dealing with her sooty chimney. One evening the previous week she had stuck the big yard brush up the chimney and brought down as much soot as she could get at. Then she put me on top of a rusty tar barrel and I climbed on to the roof, clinging on to the old brown thatch. She handed me up a furze bush and I crawled along the thatch, avoiding the sagging bits and dragging the bush after me. When I reached the chimney I stood up shakily beside it, almost afraid to look down in case I would get a reeling in my head and take a nosedive. When I had got my balance I held on to the chimney top and peered down inside. It was a black, black world down there. I dragged the furze bush over the edge of the chimney and pushed it down as far as I could and then let go, hoping that it would continue on its journey. But Nell's sooty chimney defied the laws of gravity and the furze got stuck halfway between Nell and me. She stood below looking up at the furze bush and I stood above looking down, but neither of us could reach it.

"What are we going to do now?" I called down the hollow chimney.

"Let me alone, child, I'm thinking," she shouted back at me, her voice muffled in the black interior of the chimney.

While Nell was thinking I sat on the thatch beside her chimney and picked the furze thorns out of my fingers. Then I began to appreciate my roof-top surroundings. At home I would never have been allowed to do interesting jobs like this one, and even though I was a bit scared on top of the roof, I was still thrilled to bits to be up there. Danger never crossed Nell's mind and that was one of the reasons why doing things with Nell was so exciting. I was amazed at how far across the countryside I could see from this vantage point. The school looked small away across the valley, and I could see the little stone bridge with the river disappearing beneath it and then glinting again in the distance before it crept into the wood.

"Are you still up there?" Nell's voice came through like a spirit from a dungeon. I stood up and peered down the chimney. Away below me, beneath the branches of the furze bush, I could detect movement. Because Nell's hair was black and her face a matching tone, there was no colour contrast to outline her in the sooty interior of the chimney. From where I stood everything, including Nell, was varying shades of black, and in the midst of all this valley of mourning the thorny bush was wedged.

"Stay where you are," she called up to me, and I wondered where did she think I was going to go.

"Why don't you light the fire and burn out the bush?" I shouted down at her.

"Child, you haven't a splink of sense," she told me and I did not like to tell her that my father often said the same about herself. "I'll bring in the tar barrel," she continued, "and stand on top of it and maybe I could reach the bush then."

She appeared out in the yard below. Though Nell's appearance had never been Persil white, she was now covered in loose soot that fell like a black shower around her as she bent to roll the barrel into the kitchen. At this stage all Nell's cats had decided that the fireplace was a danger zone and were stalking in protest around the yard, emitting loud wailing meows and waving their tails in the air. Her sheep dog, Shep, heavy in pup, sat with her snout along her outstretched paws, rolling the whites of her eyes, wondering what all the fuss was about. Nell had not wanted Shep to have pups and had guarded her with great vigilance, but she must have slipped up at some stage because Shep a few weeks previously had developed a pregnant appearance. Nell believed that it was Dan's mongrel who had cracked her security net and vowed vengeance, but I was thrilled with the forthcoming event and every evening after school came across the fields to Nell's house to check on Shep's progress. I wanted the pups to arrive in time for Christmas.

Nell mounted the tar barrel, but still the bush could not be reached. Nell was not easily defeated and came up with another plan. She went into her stone cow-house and came out with a ball of binder-twine.

"Catch this," she instructed, sending the ball flying in my direction, expecting me to go up for it like a Kerry mid-fielder. As I was no Mick O'Connell with a high reach, the ball of twine sailed over the roof of the house into the bushes in the grove behind.

"Child," she told me, "I'm crucified from you."

To my mind it was hard to know who was being crucified.

She disappeared into the grove and emerged triumphant with the twine. "Now this time will you catch it," she instructed.

"Don't shoot it so high," I told her, balancing myself in case I'd take a tumble down into the yard. This time her aim was so accurate that the ball hit the chimney top and before I could grasp it disappeared down the chimney. She had scored a hole in one.

"What kind of hands have you, child?" she demanded. "You wouldn't catch my donkey if he decided to fly."

I looked down the chimney and there below I could see the ball of twine tucked into the furze bush like a bird's nest. Nell, I decided, had the makings of a great full-forward – her aim was deadly.

"Now, child," she called up from below, waving another ball of twine that she had collected from the cowhouse, "this is our last chance because I've no more hay twine."

This time I was ready for her and caught it in full flight but in my anxiety to capture the ball I forgot my precarious position and nearly overbalanced off the roof.

"Child," Nell admonished from below, "will you straighten up and not be doing the fool."

"Nell," I protested, "I could have fallen down and broken my neck."

"What would you be doing that for?" she asked in annoyance.

With the ball of twine grasped firmly in my hand I held on to the side of the chimney and awaited further instructions.

"Let one end of the twine down the chimney," I was instructed, "and try to angle it in an open space in the bush," Nell shouted up at me before turning into the house. I did as I was told and passed the end of the twine down the chimney; mercifully it continued to descend until I felt a tug and Nell called with satisfaction: "I have it! Now unroll the twine and let down the other end through a different bit of the bush." This was easier said than done and it took much angling and swaying back and forth to get it where we wanted it. Even then it got stuck going down and had to be hauled back up again several times before we finally made it to the bottom. The rest was up to Nell. She now had the two ends in her hands and as she exerted pressure the bush gradually came away, carrying the soot before it.

I heard muffled grunts from the lower regions and called down to Nell: "Are you all right?"

"My tonsils and eyeballs are covered in soot," she croaked up at me.

I crawled down along the roof, holding on for dear life, and felt the wet thatch soaking up through the knees of my heavy, black, ribbed stockings. I aimed for the general direction of where I thought the tar barrel was and then slid down holding firmly on to the end of the thatch and swinging my legs, feeling for a foothold. But there was no tar barrel. I had miscalculated and now my legs were dangling in mid air.

"Nell!" I screamed. "Nell, Nell!"

After a few minutes she came around the corner of the house rolling the tar barrel. I had forgotten that she had taken it into the kitchen. "Why the dickens didn't you wait to come down on the tar barrel?" she demanded, rolling it in under my feet.

"Nell, I couldn't see from above that the barrel was not there," I told her.

"How could it be out here when I had it inside?" she complained.

"I forgot that," I said.

"Aren't I the lucky woman not to be cursed with children," she told me.

When we went back into the kitchen I came to a standstill at the doorway in amazement. "Nell, it's like the hobs of hell," I said in delight.

"Will you make yourself useful," she told me, "and start brushing it out so that the cats can come in."

We spent the rest of the evening getting rid of the soot, and by the time darkness fell we were back in action with a huge fire roaring up the chimney. So even though my father did not know it, Nell's chimney had very little need of Black Ned.

Now, a week later, as I arrived into Nell's yard with the holly, there was no trace of Shep, which was unusual, but I was so intent on my mission to decorate her house that I forgot to pursue the matter. Nell was not over-enthuastic about having her house decorated, but because I promised that I would remove everything after Christmas I gave her no grounds for opposition.

"Christmas is only for children and fools," she told me, and then she chuckled and added: "Maybe for that reason we both qualify."

The highlight of Nell's Christmas as far as I was concerned was the parcel she got from relatives in America, and it amazed me that Nell's relations could be so out of touch with her requirements. They sent her things that were beautiful and useless, but because Nell never parted with anything they were all put to some use. The previous Christmas a low-cut, white nightdress had arrived, wrapped in soft white tissue papers and smelling of exotic perfume. Nell had put the nightdress around the top of the milk churn and used it for straining the milk.

As I put up the holly I spotted strange wrapping on top of the settle, empty of whatever it had contained.

"Nell," I said gleefully, "it's after coming."

"What?" she asked innocently.

"You know what," I protested; "the parcel."

"Oh, that," she said dismissively; "full of old rubbish."

"But what was in it?" I demanded, even though I doubted that she would tell me.

An amused smile covered her face and she laughed

out loud. "You won't believe it," she chuckled.

"Believe what?" I demanded.

"What came in the parcel."

"What, what?" I demanded, jumping with excitement. Nell rarely told what came in the parcel so it had to be something very different.

"A fur coat," she gasped between splutters.

"A fur coat!" I exclaimed, flabbergasted. Nobody in our corner of the world owned a fur coat except visiting "Yanks" and the doctor's wife. Fur coats were regarded as the ultimate in high-class living. If you had a fur coat you had it made as far as we were concerned.

"Nell, what are you going to do with it?" I wanted to know.

"I'll wear it going to bed on cold nights," she told me.

"You're only codding me," I protested.

"Well," she admitted, "I found another use for it in the meanwhile."

"Where is it ?" I demanded.

"You'll find out in due course," was all the information I could get out of her. When Nell decided to close down communications it was useless to persist, so I gave up and concentrated on the holly while Nell went out to feed the hens. Usually when she did this Shep came back in with her but that evening there was no sign of her.

"Where is Shep?" I asked.

"You nearly forgot her with the holly and the parcel," she accused.

"I did nearly," I admitted.

"There is a surprise for you in the duck-house," Nell said.

"She's had the pups!" I yelled in delight and made for the door. I ran across the yard to the duck-house, a tiny lean-to attached to the cow-house. Even I had to stoop slightly to get in. There inside was Shep, thumping her tail in welcome and surrounded by her new puppies. At first I thought that there were dozens of them, but once my eyes grew accustomed to the semi-darkness of the house I realised that not all the surrounding fur was alive. Under Shep and her six puppies was Nell's new fur coat and they were stretched out enjoying its warmth and comfort. They were ready for Christmas, paw-deep in real fur.

In From the Fields

WHEN THE NIGHTS turned cold and mornings arrived wearing frosty coats, it was time to bring the heifers up from the river where they had run free for the entire summer. They had forgotten the barriers of house life and were now in a semi-wild condition, so it was all hands on deck for this major undertaking. With my father and Martin leading the way, we headed down the fields to the river valley.

Martin, who worked with us on the farm, was not much older than my brother and was full of good humour and fun. He loved singing and dancing and played the melodeon like a bird. He was a great asset when we were bringing the heifers up from the river as he calmed the situation when temperatures started to rise. When my father lost his cool it never bothered Martin and sometimes he even got a fit of laughing in the middle of one of my father's rampages. Slow-moving, morose people got on my father's nerves, but because Martin was light-hearted and quick-thinking my father was very fond of him.

My mother alone was allowed to opt out of the undertaking, pleading that she was not able to run fast enough, and we could not argue with that excuse. The ability to outrun these long-legged, fit young heifers was essential; sometimes we were convinced that several of them had Grand National possibilities. At first we formed a large semi-circle around them and edged them gently towards the first gap and they came along demurely enough, but as they were gradually eased out of familiar territory into strange fields they closed ranks into an uneasy pack, sensing trouble ahead. We held our distance to avoid exciting them, but still guided them in the right direction by waving our hands if they made a wrong turning.

Gradually they gathered speed and huddled together in a head-to-tail line, and we knew from experience that they were watching the chance for one of them to make a break for freedom. Sometimes it would be the leader of the pack, but it might be any one of them back along the line, so we had to be prepared for flight from any angle, for if one of them broke ranks there would be no holding the rest of them. My father believed that family history had to be taken into consideration when anticipating trouble.

"Watch that small black bitch – her grandmother always had her head up looking for trouble," he shouted.

Two of us ran ahead to block off possible avenues of escape and all went well until we reached the field below the house and they saw the farmyard. Some instinct warned them that they were losing their freedom and they decided that this far and no further would they go. Instead of one of them making a drive for freedom as we had anticipated, three of them made a bid for it simultaneously.

"Stop that bloody rip!" my father shouted at me when a heifer, rolling the whites of her eyes, tried to trample me underfoot. "Don't let her get away," he yelled, impervious to the fact that he might wind up minus one daughter. I stood my ground, waving a branch desperately under her nose, trying to convince her that I would not be moved. She backed off at the last minute, just when I was beginning to think that she was going to give me a free ride on her horns.

We succeeded in holding two of them, but the small black one, as my father had warned, had generations of revolutionary blood in her veins. She broke through and headed back down to the river with her tail flying high. She was called the Blackbird after her mother and a line of grandmothers, and watching her in full flight one could only conclude that she was well named. My father sent such a litany of curses after her that if they had had the power to ignite she would have been cremated on the spot.

"Follow her," he called to my brother, the proud owner of many medals for being fleet of foot, who now tested his athletic skill against the Blackbird. She had a head start but he had more brains. He took a short-cut across one field and when she reached the bottom gap he was there before her, much to her amazement, so she turned tail and headed back up towards us. On her return she shot into the middle of the herd, breathing heavily and tossing her head, which had the effect of sending charges of nervous tension through the rest of them. All it would take now was one false move to send them stampeding in all directions. They were throbbing with excitement and fear of the unknown.

"Don't excite them!" my father shouted furiously and immediately had just that effect. We waited for them to steady down a bit and then eased them through the gate into the haggard; the cow-house door was straight ahead of them now, but how to convince them to put their heads through it was the problem. The only way was to form a human chain around them and give them no other avenue of escape, but there was no guarantee that any minute they might not decide to either break the human chain or simply jump over it. Slowly we edged them forward. We were almost there and all our nerves were stetched to breaking-point when suddenly a cat shot out the door against them. The terrified heifers bolted in all directions and we scattered before them like straw in the wind.

"Jesus, Mary and holy St Joseph," my father prayed, "where did that frigger of a cat come from?"

Some of us had slipped on our flight before the heifers, so now knees and backsides were many shades of green, but the predominant colour was fresh, smelly green as excited cattle are prone to frequency in both bowel and urinary tract. We were back to square one but we were even a degree worse because now the cattle were scared stiff and instead of being in a herd were all over the farmyard. Martin decided then that we should take them in smaller groups and I was warned by my father to lock up the whole cat family or he would strangle every one of the bastards with his bare hands. After that we took them in pairs, and once we had the first two in, the rest fell into line easily enough. Finally they were all installed, much to our relief.

The heifers were the last animals to be brought in from the fields before Christmas. Now the sheep alone remained outside, but they had big, warm, fleece-lined coats to keep out the cold and every evening hay was carried down the fields to them. After a few days the heifers fell into routine with the other cattle and went willingly into the stalls where sweet-smelling hay awaited them every night. The haggard across the wall had a barn full of hay to feed them throughout the winter. In a yard below the barn the horses, James and Paddy, stood in the stable and hay was thrown in the window above their heads and fell into their mangers. Beyond the stables the pig-houses were empty except for the old sows. All the others had been fattened and sent to O'Meara's Meat factory in Limerick, and the cheque from their sale would keep us going over the winter. Two of them had been killed for home consumption and were now in timber barrels of pickle in the lower room or hanging off the meat-hooks from the kitchen ceiling. The hams were up the chimney being smoked for Christmas.

On the farm in the winter there was very little income, but since we were fairly self-sufficient it took little to keep us going. The hens sometimes obliged and a few of them kept laying even during the cold weather. One cow kept us in milk and she was called "the stripper". She was not in calf and she continued to provide milk over the Christmas period while her pregnant sisters were resting. What was drawn from her was described as "the strippings", which was a term also used to describe the first of the milk drawn off the udder of ordinary cows before the milking proper commenced. There was very little milk in either case.

With all the animals housed for the winter it was time to tidy things up out in the yard for the Christmas. Martin was due to go home on Christmas Eve, so he and my brother spent the last few days brushing the haggard, the cow-yard and the passageways. It was a mucky job but it was all part of the Christmas clean-up. It was our job when they had their part done to tackle the walls. First we washed them down with buckets of water and then used the kitchen brush to wash away their green slimy look. The water was cold and the day was cold and by the time the job was done our hands showed a mixed colour scheme of navy and purple. When the walls were dry we mixed lime in a big tin bath where it frothed and spat as the first of the hot water hit it. My mother cautioned about not getting lime in our eyes but it always seemed to happen and some unfortunate ran to the kitchen crying for water and a towel to repair the damage. We had to get the whitewash to the right consistency. Too thick and progress was slowed down; too thin and the yard was whitewashed by the overflow, which could lead to some very derisory comments from people who considered themselves expert colour consultants. When the mix was judged right, we added a squeeze from my mother's blue bag, and here we had to be careful because white walls were the requirement, not blue ones, but a squirt of blue gave them a brilliant white look. We got to work with two big whitewashing brushes and covered all before us, even bits of the hedge that came in our way. The end result was glorious and brightened up the whole dark winter's day. The hen-house, the turf-house, and the pig's house all got a lick. They lost their green mottled look and were almost brighter than white.

Between the main farmyard and our garden was a long low wall with a hedge hanging out over it and this wall, together with the two small pillars, had to be cement-washed. A less dramatic job, so less desirable, it nevertheless had to be done. We were not supposed to paint the garden gate, but there was green paint still left in the tin since the last Stations, so we sneaked it out and the gate became bright green in minutes. My mother objected to painting the gate in the winter and we discovered why when my father came swearing into the kitchen that night holding up two green hands for all to see.

Cleaning Up

DURING THE DAYS leading up to Christmas I sometimes wondered if Santa was a hygiene inspector. My sisters started clean-up operations in the upstairs bedrooms: they stripped down all the beds and turned the horsehair mattresses and feather ticks. Showers of feathers often rose into the air during these undertakings, which meant that a hole in the tick had to be located and stitched up. Sometimes it was the pillows that were at fault and it was amazing the quantity of feathers and down that could make its way out through a tiny tear. The marathon bed overhaul resulted in tubs of washing, but the days were wild and windy so they came in fairly dry in the evenings. At night my mother turned the backs of the chairs to the fire and linked the sheets along them for airing. I loved the smell of sheets airing around the fire and sometimes crept in under them to savour the warm, clean smell of drying linen and cotton. The first night that these went on the beds they smelt of the world outside and the peaty essence of the turf fire.

Once the beds had been done, the upstairs floors were next in line. Some had bare boards and others were lino-covered and all had to be scrubbed down with a tin bucket of hot soapy water. A big tin of Mansion's floor polish was rubbed into the lino with a discarded vest and then we started to shine with an old soft knickers under each foot. We shot back and forth along the floors, pretending that we were on a skating rink and rising a great shine. Polishing the landing and stairs was outlawed because the previous Christmas my father had taken off on the top step of the stairs to make a crash landing at the bottom. His stockinged feet had shot him smoothly and silently over the edge, but that had been the only smooth and silent thing about the whole performance. He had arrived toes-first into the kitchen at such a speed that he overshot the runway and did not grind to a halt until he was half-way across the kitchen floor. Our Lady and St Joseph and every saint in heaven were called to witness the fact that he could have been maimed for life as a result of the madness of a house full of women with nothing better to occupy them than polishing steps with the sole intent of killing everyone who went up and down them!

Cleaning the upstairs windows was an exercise in acrobatics – and a chilly exercise, as you had to hang out of the window to get at the outside. The windows were small and did not run freely, some having been stuck solid for years, so you had to lean out where possible and then squirm around like a snail to reach awkward corners. Sometimes a blade had to be brought into action where the painter of the previous summer had left a smear down the sides. When the entire bedroom clean-up had been finished, it was a pleasure to open the door at the foot of the stairs at night and get the fresh smell of floor polish wafting down against you.

Downstairs was where the real marathon took place. Our kitchen ceiling consisted of a series of long, narrow ceiling laths which had been painted cream, but during the year the smoke had changed the colour to a tawny beige. We pulled the two kitchen tables into key positions and mounted them, with scrubbing brushes and buckets of warm soapy water. Water ran down our arms and up our sleeves as we worked, but after a long strug-

gle some of the smoke effects were eradicated. Before the scrubbing could commence we had had to take down the pieces of bacon hanging off the ceiling hooks and these now had to be heaved up again. As for the kitchen walls, the lower half, which we called "the partition", was lined with timber and had to be washed down, while the wall above it was distempered a pale yellow.

At the bottom of the kitchen stood a big cream-coloured press with two glass doors; beneath them were two large drawers and two solid doors at the bottom. The top shelves of this deep press held the everyday kitchen ware, with slats along the back for big plates; the bottom section was the food store cupboard. One drawer in between held the cutlery and the other was the receiver of homeless objects. Before Christmas the entire contents of the press were laid out all over the kitchen, and it was almost impossible to find a temporary home for everything. But once the oilcloth lining of the press had been washed clean with the ever-reliable Vim, everything could be returned to base. The biggest upheaval was caused by the removal from the press of the big brown and blue dishes that were supported by a timber bar running midway along the top shelf. We had to be careful when taking them out because often things poked in behind them collapsed with their removal. When replacing them my mother cautioned about banging the dishes off each other and chipping them. Some were very old, having been in the house before herself, and she wanted them to survive to the next generation. She regarded with great respect everything that had been in the house when she had come into it; though a lover of people rather than things, she still felt that articles handed down from previous generations possessed a special value, so even though Grand-mother Taylor had been dead with many years we treated her dishes with the utmost care when doing our Christmas clean-up.

A further problem was posed by the dumping drawer because it was creaking at the seams with homeless objects. Nobody wanted the job of dealing with it because it put you in a no-win situation. You had to get rid of some of the contents, but no matter how discerning you were there were going to be repercussions and retributions. In there were torn table-books, broken crayons, old creamery books, red copies of the *Messenger*, brass door-knobs and – most important of all – old letters. Years afterwards, when I had left home, the first thing I always did on returning was to go to that drawer and rummage through its contents to read all the family letters that had come in my absence. In many ways it represented the pulse of the home. The first time I found myself in the position of not being free to do so, I knew

that home was no longer quite home anymore.

Whitewashing the hob for Christmas required a special effort. After removing the big iron kettles and hangers the crane was swung outwards into the kitchen. The goose-wing was used to brush down the turf dust all around the hearth and out from behind the bellows. In there was the home of the cricket who was seldom seen but often heard as he provided our nightly background music around the fire.

The whitewash was made extra-thick and creamy, and as we went into every crevice we peered up at the hams where they were hanging off the brad above our heads. When the hob was gleaming white on either side of the black smoke trail up the centre, the crane was brushed down with an old scrubbing brush and then swung back into position. Across the chimney breast the oilcloth kept in the smoke and formed a decorative overhead boundary between the kitchen and the hearth, but last year's oilcloth was cracked and its serrated edges had curled up from the effects of the heat and old age, so the old one was removed and a new one, glossy green and red, was tacked on.

One job that we all tried to avoid in the Christmas clean-up was the task of reducing my father's butter box to manageable proportions. It was his tool box, but he never saw the need to tidy it up and throw away the rubbish; he kept piling stuff in until it overflowed and poured out on to the surrounding floor. The contents of the box were dirty and rusty and by the time you had it sorted out your fingernails were broken and your hands filthy. And if my father walked in while you were at it you could finish up dead. When we could postpone the job no longer we threw the contents out on to the floor and what we thought he needed we threw back in as fast as possible; all the little bits of timber that were causing most of the clutter we threw into the fire. The first time he had to use it after this clean-out, we all disappeared!

The windows were next in line. When we pulled out the shutters we were greeted with a shower of dust and some loose mortar. Cobwebs were draped between the loose stones, and as their creators ran for cover we saw the evidence that this was a main road for travelling mice. Because our house was old its thick walls afforded shelter for lives other than ours and sometimes these parallel lives intruded on each other. Now we removed signs of others' occupancy and closed back the shutters; they could live in peace for another twelve months. Then we washed down the shutters and polished the windows, the front one getting special attention because that window-sill would be the home of the Christmas candle.

CLEANING UP

The closing scene in the Christmas clean-up was the scrubbing of the two timber tables and the *súgán** chairs before we got to the grand finale of the floor. If it was a fine day we carried the chairs to the spout at the end of the garden and stood them into the running stream where we scrubbed away in the cold water. As we carried the chairs up through the garden back to the kitchen door a poem from our school book came into my mind; it was called "The Table and The Chair".

Said the table to the chair,
"You can hardly be aware
How I suffer from the heat
And the chilblains on my feet!
If we took a little walk
We might have a little talk!
Pray let us take the air!"
Said the table to the chair.

Said the chair unto the table,
"Now you know we are not able!
How foolishly you talk
When you know we cannot walk!"
Said the table with a sigh,
"It can do no harm to try;
I've as many legs as you,
Why can't we walk on two?"

Our chairs were a mismatched bunch with high backs and low backs, with *súgán* seats and timber seats, and because they were all unique I always felt that each one received you differently. At Christmas these chairs were joined by an armchair from the parlour. There was a mad rush for the privilege of sitting in this over the Christmas period, but my father had first claim, so

* chairs with rope seats

when he was present that finished all arguments. As well as the armchair, into the kitchen came a one-armed leather sofa, and over this my mother threw one of the warm trap rugs, and there was also a great scramble for a place on this. The kitchen floor was washed with buckets of water, and as soon as it had dried out the scrubbed tables and chairs were brought back in and then the visiting furniture from the parlour was brought down. The two parlour pieces gave the kitchen a different look. It somehow looked as if we were expecting important visitors. But there was one more thing to be brought from the parlour to the kitchen for Christmas and that was the gramophone. To us it was the most important item of all, but it could not be brought down until Christmas Eve when all the decorations were up.

Bringing the Christmas

WHEN THE LEAVES began to fall, we drew the turf home from the bog. Every year my father declared that he would do it earlier the following year, but despite all his good intentions it always seemed to run late. Sometimes he hired a rickety old lorry belonging to Janey Jack Owen who lived across the river. I loved to sit on the red leather seat high up in the cab which gave me a great view out over surrounding ditches so that I could see fields and houses that I had never seen before. The seat bounced up and down with the bumps in the road and the hammers and wrenches that were strewn around beneath our feet rattled noisily in harmony with all the other creakings of the old lorry. Janey Jack Owen was dark and handsome and it fascinated me to watch his brown hands pull the big lorry into position. A drive in a lorry was a whole new experience for me and Janey Jack Owen, with his black boiler suit that smelt of oil and petrol, brought a new dimension to our country living. But more often the turf was drawn home by the jennet and crib. Our jennet was the only unchristened animal on the farm; he was just the jennet, a bit like the Taoiseach, the President or the Queen. He did not like the long trips to the bog, but at least it signalled that the year's work was beginning to wind down and his daily trips to the creamery would soon be phased out.

Once the turf had arrived into the yard, it was our job to stack it into an old stone house with a sloping galvanised iron roof. We arranged a conveyor belt system whereby two of us flung the sods in the door and two others stacked it against the back wall, working forwards. The aim of the two out in the yard was to make life as uncomfortable as possible for the two stackers by hopping as many sods as possible off them, and sometimes sods came back out in retaliation. Finally, when we came to the end of the load, the broken turf that we called "ciarans" was piled up in the corner and also the really tiny bits called the "brus" that were very good for lighting the fire. When the house was full my father built a reek with the remaining loads and thatched it with straw.

Our house was surrounded by trees, and winter storms brought some of the old ones down, so before Christmas my father brought out the long cross-cut saw and, having cornered a victim to pull the saw with him, he got to work. Then the tree lengths had to be split with a sledge and wedges and finally made smaller again with a hatchet. After that we piled the wood up at the end of the house where it was a sign that Christmas was around the corner and an insurance policy against the cold winter. When my father was splitting the logs, we kept an eye out for a really nice-looking log that would be the right length and would fit snugly across the back of our open fire. It had to be just right because it would be our Christmas log, or "Blockeen na Nollag" as my grandmother called it. The final selection made, it was hidden at the back of the pile in case some uninformed adult might split it up into ordinary logs.

Beside the reek of turf my father made a pit for the potatoes and this was also covered with straw against the frost. Here, too, was the pit for the mangles and turnips – the mangles for the horses and the turnips for kitchen consumption. The finest turnip to pass through his hands was put aside for the Christmas candle.

As he pitted the potatoes he filled four bags to be taken with the geese to town relations: Golden Wonders for Aunty Maggie because she had always liked them when she had shared house with my father before he got married, and Kerr's Pinks for Cousin Nonie because she lived alone and considered Golden Wonders too big for her saucepan. He always complained about Cousin Nonie's choice of potatoes: "Bloody woman – reared in the country and now with a pot too small for a decent spud. What is the world coming to?" Despite his complaints he still filled the bags and lined them up against the stone wall of the small house at the end of the garden where the geese were already swinging from the rafters. Beside them he put a bag of turnips for Aunty Maggie, who got special attention because my father had a soft spot for her.

With the money from the goose market in her handbag, my mother started to make preparations early on the day that they were going to town to bring home the Christmas. First, the four chosen geese were brought to the kitchen where she wrapped them in white flour bags for the journey. She was always in a dilemma as to whether she should clean out the geese before delivery. She believed that the geese kept better if they remained intact until the day before Christmas, but on the other hand she felt that the recipients were more appreciative of a goose minus innards. My father cut short her deliberations by informing her how lucky they were to be getting a goose in the first place and if they were too damn lazy to clean her out then that was their problem. The next item on the agenda was the allocation of the geese: my mother felt that Cousin Nonie should get the best plucked goose because she was so fussy, whereas the general consensus was that for that precise reason she should not. My mother's head and heart were often in conflict, but my father had no such qualms, and the better he liked, the more he gave.

With each goose she placed a big brown bastable cake, and eventually everything, including my father's potatoes and turnips, was stored in the cart behind the jennet. Much to his annoyance the jennet was brought out of hibernation for this trip to town, and he relieved his frustration by stretching out his long neck and trying to sink his teeth into anyone unwise enough to come within biting distance. He knew nothing about the spirit of Christmas or good will to all men. He only knew that while the horses, James and Paddy, were inside in the warm comfortable stables nuzzling each other's necks, he was out in the cold tackled up for work. It was well known in town that "Taylor's jennet" had to be kept at a safe distance, and whenever he stood tethered to a pole along the street he was given a wide berth by passers-by. His hooded eyes were always on the look-out for a likely victim. He would stand by the side of the street with his head down, pretending to be asleep, waiting for the unwary who ventured too close, and when absent-minded pedestrians came along he would whip his long jaw in their direction and sample an elbow, if he got them in time, or a bottom if they were moving away. Giving a kick was another of the joys of his life and he had the ability to swing his leg at extraordinary angles – indeed, he seemed to have the makings of a great set dancer.

Before they finally left the house my father went upstairs to visit the money-box, which was always kept locked in a big brown timber trunk, the small silver key to which was either in my father's pocket or behind the dish in the ware press. We were never allowed to put a finger into the trunk, but on rare occasions my mother could be persuaded to allow us a quick look. In it were old photograph albums, the christening robe, a watch that my mother had got from her mother, and her engagement ring. There were many other boxes in there that I always wanted to investigate, but my father maintained that in a house full of children there should be some corner safe from destructive little fingers. It was my idea of heaven to put my nose in over the edge of that trunk, to just breathe deeply and absorb its aroma. It smelt of tobacco, soft leather and old papers, because in there were family wills, deeds and documents, and in the middle of them all was the brown tin money-box. Into this during the year went the proceeds from the sale of farm animals and the fruits of the farm. The money was kept in different rolls and each roll was earmarked for a different cause, but the most important roll was reserved for paying Martin. He started on the first of February and finished on Christmas Eve and his wages were seventy pounds for the whole year. Often it worried my father that he might not be able to make the sum, and all through the year out of every sale of calves and bonhams, so much was put into Martin's little bundle.

Now my father opened up the brown tin box and took out a roll of red twenty pound notes. Today in town he would pay all the shops that had supplied us during the year. As he packed the roll of notes into the top pocket of his waistcoat I stood beside him to sniff their special smell. To me those big red notes represented riches beyond measure. While my father was collecting his money, my mother was rounding up her shopping bags, and when all was in order the last item to go in to the cart was a big double-department box of eggs. The money from these, together with the goose money, would help my mother to bring the Christmas.

As they set off on their journey we all stood at the gate and watched them go. We accepted the fact that there was no question of any of us accompanying them, but though we remained at home we went with them in spirit. We knew that my father's first port of call was to Jack, who provided everything that we wore throughout the year. He wrote it all into a big leather ledger and today he would have it all added up because he knew that the farmers all came to town before Christmas to clear their slates. The amount of this bill always took my father unawares, for no matter how much he expected it to be it always turned out to be more. He could never understand how it could cost so much to keep us all under cover, even though the bill only included bare necessities as my mother and grandmother made most of our clothes. Then he called to Ned's, where we got our weekly messages, and then to the store that supplied the feeding for the pigs and bran for the cows and horses. His last port of call was the pub, but it was more than a pub because amongst other things Tom sold gramophone records. Here my father purchased new records for Christmas and a box of new brass gramophone needles. As Tom packed a box with bottles of porter and red lemonade, my father sat by the fire with others who were on the same mission and they shared a seasonal drink and discussed the year that was almost gone, while their wives shopped for the Christmas. There, too, he met his Uncle Andy who was a widower and usually came home with him to spend Christmas with us.

In every shop my mother called to on the day, she was presented with a token of appreciation of her custom through the year. These Christmas boxes really put the gloss on our Christmas and varied from big, soft barm bracks and seed loaves to boxes of biscuits and sometimes even an iced cake. Bringing the Christmas included necessities as well as luxuries, and so part of my mother's shopping consisted of a chest of tea and a sack of brown and white flour. Normally my father and the jennet brought such necessities daily when going to the creamery, but with that journey cancelled for the winter provisions had to be bought. If the snow came long and heavy we could be cut off from the town for a lengthy period, and so, like the squirrel, we stored up supplies for the season.

When my mother had her shopping done she met up with my father in Tom's and together they went to distribute the geese and potatoes to the relations. Finally they loaded up the purchases. The last thing to be put on board was a gallon of paraffin oil for the lamps and the wet battery for the radio to keep us in touch with the outside world.

When we heard them coming into the yard that night we nearly knocked each other down as we ran out the door to help them bring in the Christmas. We welcomed Uncle Andy with delight and swung off him, and he tousled our hair and said to each of us, "Hello, Bobba." The sacks of flour were brought in first and, because they had to be stored in a dry place, the timber bin beside the fire was wiped out and the billowing flour was poured in. Then the chest of tea was taken to the bedroom over the kitchen, which was the dryest. After that my mother was very careful that we did not get to look into some boxes, but we were satisfied to see the big Christmas candles and to hear the lemonade gurgling in the bottles. The records, however, we were allowed to inspect and we poured into the parlour and surrounded the gramophone on the end of the old sideboard. We were cautioned to be careful and not to scratch the records and the caution was necessary because our record collection included a few croaking tenors who had been scratched out of recognition. Uncle Andy decided that records were no substitute for a live performance and we all returned to the kitchen to watch him dance a jig, the few pints that he had consumed in town giving height to his step. We always loved it when he came for Christmas because he was light-hearted and full of fun – and he was the only one who could boss my father, which was a great plus as far as we were concerned. From his inside pocket my father pulled a green-covered copy of *Old Moore's Almanac* which was to be consulted throughout the year for prophecies of weather and disasters; but for now he stuck it behind one of the stair banisters because Uncle Andy was busy entertaining us with the the most enjoyable extracts from the more festive-looking *Holly Bough*.

While Uncle Andy entertained us in the kitchen my mother had gone into the parlour where she stowed away parcels in the press beside the fireplace. Now at last Christmas was almost here, because it was locked into the big press, ready to emerge on Christmas Eve.

The Gates of Heaven

I SAT ON a low *súgán* chair beside Mrs Casey's fire and watched her making her Christmas cake. The flames from her big turf fire curled up around the bottom of her black iron kettle, which was sending steam signals up the chimney and almost obliterating the crane overhead. Mrs Casey was getting the fire ready for her last Christmas baking session and she wanted it glowing and settled and the kettle boiling beside it so that she could make her tea without disturbing the bastable, which would shortly replace the kettle on the hangers over the fire.

Our house stood on the side of a hill looking down over a valley; a long, winding boreen sloped up to the old road above and Mrs Casey's cottage was along that road. My father always referred to being "up at the road" when he called in to see Mrs Casey. We never passed her cottage on our way home from town without calling in to see her. Her family had grown up and gone; as she used to say herself: "the chickens have left the nest". But she did not suffer from an entirely empty nest since we regarded her as a second mother who was always on hand to dish out both practical and philosophical advice. For me she had solved the problem of where babies came from; my mother had given me a limited explanation but, being thirsty for every minute detail, I had gone to Mrs Casey and she had given me a full, unabridged version. She loved children and men, and regarded women as sisters in the battle of survival and child-bearing. "Give a married woman her full title," she used to say; "she has it earned." She dealt with the two great realities of life – birth and death – because she both delivered the babies and also laid out the dead. A corner-stone in our daily lives, she was never known to anybody by any name other than Mrs Casey.

A small, creaking gate opened from the old road into the short, narrow pathway that led to her cottage. A high hedge arched over the pathway with a little opening on one side into her crowded garden, and a timber gate on the right led into her haggard, which was a hive of industry with a stall for two cows, a stable for the pony and a shed for hens and ducks. On her dresser in the kitchen during the summer there was always a big white enamel bucket full of eggs. As the weather grew colder the egg supply decreased and Mrs Casey had to threaten and coax her hens to continue laying and subscribe to her Christmas baking.

Her ample figure almost obliterated the light coming in through the small, deep window over the table where she was busy cracking eggs into a white basin. It was a big table which ran the length of the wall behind the door as you came into her kitchen. The dresser was on the wall opposite and the pony's collar hung over the open fireplace which extended along the gable end wall of the cottage. She always had a fine fire going, with her dog Bran stretched out in front of it and her husband Jack busy turning the bellows to keep the flames jumping. Today, however, there was no Jack to be seen.

"Once he had the fire right, I sent him to town for a few pints to keep him out of my way," she explained. She had a smiling face with two rosy cheeks and her white hair was tied in a knot at the back of her head. When she laughed, which was often, she threw back her head and great peals of laughter filled the kitchen

as her short, blocky body shook with merriment. She was my idea of what Santa Claus would look like if he was a woman and she had a great big heart which made her very suitable for the job. She wore a long black skirt down to her toes and when she went to town she wrapped a black shawl around her shoulders.

Now the shawl hung off a hook on the back of the door; she had on a dark red blouse, the sleeves rolled up, and her sturdy arms were buried in flour. Scattered around the table were basins of sugar, whipped eggs, cream and Ned's muscatel raisins. Mrs Casey worked by instinct and threw handfuls of different ingredients into the tin baking pan. On the window-sill stood a redundant cookery book which had lost its cover years previously and was illustrated by years of egg-yolk and butter staining. It was propped up by a bottle of porter but was never consulted, for Mrs Beaton was just the

guardian angel of the Christmas baking.

When Mrs Casey had the cake almost ready, she swung the kettle off the hangers and replaced it with the black bastable which she tilted forward, covering the base with a light sprinkling of flour. Then she lifted the cake in her two outstretched hands and laid it into the oven and made a cross on it. Then she put on the cover and covered it with coals.

"Now," she said with satisfaction, "I think we deserve a cup of tea." She cleared a small corner of the table and we sat there to have our tea and some of her crumbly brown bread. As we ate we chatted and I told her about Nell's Shep having pups and how Nell was mad with Dan because she blamed his mongrel Prince for the unexpected litter.

"If ever a dog had an inappropriate name, that Prince has, but then Dan is an old rogue," she said indulgently.

"Nell thinks that he is a right ruffian," I told her quoting Nell's words.

"Ah, Nell," she said philosophically, "there was too much gall in her mother's milk."

This was a bit beyond me so I did not pursue the subject and asked her instead: "Mrs Casey, do you love Christmas?"

"Well, you know," she answered reflectively, "Christmas can be a sad time for people too. It's a remembering time for us older ones. We remember the people who are gone."

"Oh, I never thought of that," I told her in surprise.

"Well, that's youth for you," she said; "you don't start to look back over your shoulder until there is something to look back at, and around Christmas I tend to think of Christmases past and the people gone with them."

"Who are they?" I asked.

"Well, I suppose at Christmas the people who have gone during the year are especially with you, and then there are the people who have gone over the years – you tend to look back and think about them as well. Then I always think of Richard Brown, down the road: he had been sick for a long time and then on Christmas night I was out closing the hen-house and I looked up at the sky and saw a star falling and I knew then that he was gone to heaven and that they would be sending for me, and sure enough the son was here within the hour.

"I always remember your own grandmother," she continued, nodding her head, "old Mrs Taylor. She died on a Christmas Night."

"Oh," I said shivering, "I wouldn't like to die on a Christmas Night."

"A good night to die," she smiled; "they say that the gates of heaven are open on Christmas Night."

"I never knew that," I said in amazement.

"Yes, indeed," she said, "so your grandmother died on a holy night, as did your Uncle Barry who died in Boston a few years before her. He was the eldest of the family and he emigrated when he was very young and he never came home again – people didn't in those days, you know."

"Gee, I think that was awful sad," I said.

"Well, life was like that then," Mrs Casey said quietly, "but Barry never lost touch and he took out many of the neighbours' children who needed to go, and you couldn't go there without having somebody to more or less sponsor you. He took out one of the Lane girls down the road and she actually nursed him when he was dying. He was a young man when he died. Did your father ever tell you about the Christmas Night that he died?" she asked.

"No," I answered, my eyes glued to her face.

"Well, it was a strange night, so it was. That Lane girl who was looking after your Uncle Barry in Boston left his room to go downstairs to have something to eat while he was sleeping quietly. When she came back up he was getting back into bed, and she was amazed because he was quite weak at the time, and he said to her: 'I've been on a long, long journey.' Well, that same night down in your house your father and your Uncle Bill were sleeping up in the attic – they were only young fellows at the time. Some time during the night something woke your Uncle Bill and there was a small dark man with a beard standing at the foot of the bed. The hair stood on the top of your Uncle Bill's head and he shook your father who was in the bed with him, but when your father woke up there was nobody there. The following morning Bill told his mother about it, though your father was trying to convince him that he had dreamt it. But she questioned him about the appearance of the man. 'That was Barry,' she said. 'The description fits exactly.'"

"But why didn't Uncle Bill recognise him?"

"Well, that time the eldest was often gone before the youngest was reared, and that was the case with Bill and Barry. But I met your grandmother soon after and she was worried: 'There is something wrong beyond,' was what she said to me. She was right. Soon afterwards they got the letter saying he was dead, and when the Lane girl came home that summer, they pieced the whole story together."

After Mrs Casey finished telling her story, we were silent for a while. I wondered why Dad had never told us about Uncle Barry. He had told us that his mother had died on Christmas Night and sometimes in the middle of all the excitement of Christmas Night he would sit smoking his pipe looking into the fire, and now after hearing Mrs Casey's story I would know that the night had many memories for him.

"I'm glad you told me that story," I said.

"Good," she said, rising up off the chair. "Children should be told these things. Now we had better have a peep at this cake before himself is in on top of us."

Later, as I walked down the boreen in the dusk of the evening, I thought of what Mrs Casey had said and looked up at the sky to see if I could see a star falling. Mrs Casey was a spiritual woman and her faith was rooted deep in the earth and in the people around her, and what she had told me seemed to bring heaven and earth closer together. The people who had lived in our house down through the years belonged in our Christmas; her telling had brought them nearer, and I liked her belief that the gates of heaven were open on Christmas Night, though I had no desire to test her theory.

Christmas Eve

WHEN I OPENED my eyes the first thing I saw was the old fir tree just outside the window with a frosty shawl around her shoulders. Suddenly I knew that the long-awaited day was here at last; anticipation that had been simmering in my veins for days burst into flame with the realisation that the weeks of preparation were finally over and we were now on the threshold of Christmas. Simultaneous with the awareness of morning came a wave of euphoria flooding my mind. Before jumping out of bed I stretched to my full length under the warm quilt, letting the sheer delight penetrate every fibre of my being. A dart of excitement wiped the last traces of sleep out of my head. It was Christmas Eve at last: the essence of it was in the air, it was in the house, but most of all it was in my mind. It had built up gradually over the previous weeks since the night my mother had rounded us all up to pluck the Christmas geese.

In the bed beside me my sister's face was buried in the pillow and her long black hair streamed down over the heavy patchwork quilt that formed a bodyguard between us and the crippling cold of the bedroom. She was sound asleep and I lay beside her savouring the knowledge that Santa – who was as real to me as my old friend Bill – was packing his sleigh to begin his journey which later that night would bring him to me with the first doll that I could call my own. A new doll, not a patched-up hand-me-down from an older sister.

THE NIGHT BEFORE CHRISTMAS

This was going to be the best Christmas ever. I eased
my toe out from under the quilt but withdrew it sharply
when I felt the icy draught. The old quilt was so heavy
that you had to lift it before you could turn beneath it,
but it had a plus factor in that no chill pierced through;
to come out from under it on a cold morning was like
coming up out of a warm burrow. When I put my foot on
the ice-cold lino on the floor, I almost fell over with the
shock. I stood shivering in the arctic conditions, and because I did not want to suffer in silence, I shook my sister and breathed the magic word, "Santy". It did not
work, however, and she burrowed further down under
the quilt until she became just a bump in the middle of
the bed.

I gathered my clothes in a bundle under my arm and
sat myself down on the threadbare mat outside the bed.
It was a little oasis that lessened the stinging chill of
the hard cold floor. I pulled up my long black knitted
stockings over my thin white legs, which reminded me
of the bare branches of the winter trees, and they became the spindly black legs of my grandmother's goat.
When I had my lower half insulated, I eased off my
long flannelette nightdress and started on my top half.
As I donned the layers that my mother felt were sufficient protection against prevailing weather conditions I
watched through the frosty patterns on the window-
pane my mother, father, brother and older sisters come
in from milking the cows to their breakfast. Their
warm breath curled upwards in the air like the smoke
from my father's pipe.

When I was dressed I sat and surveyed the room with
satisfaction. It was tidier than it had been for many
months because of the overhaul the whole house had
got in preparation for Santa. Our eldest sister Frances,
who had been in charge of the clean-up operation, had

assured us that Santa was very generous to tidy children. We were not going to allow our usual clutter to curtail his giving spirit!

After breakfast my sisters and I started to decorate the kitchen. The previous day, under the direction of Frances, we had scrubbed the *súgán* chairs and wooden tables and swirled buckets of water across the stone floor. We had cleaned the windows and whitewashed the hob and now the whole kitchen was ready to be decorated; the Christmas enthusiasm that had been suppressed for weeks broke forth as we set out to decorate every corner.

My mother, however, was more concerned with practical matters and was busy filling the black pot over the fire with potatoes to be boiled for the stuffing. We had drawn several buckets of potatoes in from the potato pit the day before and washed them in an old tin bath under the spout at the end of the yard. They were now lined up in the lower room to see us over the Christmas period. While the potatoes were coming to the boil, my mother lifted the smoked ham down from the chimney and washed it with cold spring water that she had brought from the well. By the time the ham was washed, the potatoes were boiling, so she moved them sideways and the pot with the ham took centre stage.

Then she went to the turf-house and brought in a long-legged, rigid goose. It was difficult to imagine that this had been one of the plump geese who had waddled so happily around the farmyard and swum up and down the little river below the meadow just a few months before. She was laid out on the kitchen table and my mother commenced dissecting operations on her. To run your hand along her chilly leg was to discover the real meaning of "goose pimples". The first indignity she suffered was the removal of her wings and these were placed behind the bellows where the joints would dry out and season; they would then be ready for action as dust gatherers and cobweb collectors. An enamel plate was filled with methylated spirits and set alight and then the goose was moved slowly back and forth in the blue blaze to singe off her pen feathers. The singeing produced an acrid smell around the kitchen, so the window had to be opened to clear the air. The next thing the goose lost was her head and then her windpipe was yanked out. We stood around with our mouths open in horror watching all this mutilation take place but when her rear quarters were opened and multi-coloured organs were evicted we scattered. But my mother attended to this ritual with painstaking precision. The fat that lined the goose's stomach was collected and put into a jar for future use in lubricating stiff joints and softening tough leather. Her yellow legs had boiling water poured over them until the skin fell off and these, together with her neck and gizzard and other repulsive-looking bits, were put in a saucepan to simmer by the fire and form the base for tomorrow's gravy. Would I ever be able to forget where it came from?

Having abandoned our mother to the monotonous job of removing the remainder of the pen feathers by hand, we went to the turf-house to bring in the big bundle of holly. Here the other two geese still hung and I gave them a wide berth. The holly was landed in the centre of the kitchen floor, where we carefully untied the foxy binder-twine that bound it together, easing our fingers gingerly between the glossy spikes that were hell-bent on scratching us. The released bundle stretched itself across the kitchen floor, its suppressed branches arched upwards and outwards and scattered red berries in all directions, turning the kitchen into a holly garden. We set to with enthusiasm, cracking off bits of different

lengths and working it into every available corner. The fact that the ceiling had a timber cornice mould which wound all around the kitchen provided us with a ready furrow into which to poke our holly pieces, but sometimes before they were securely rooted in position a little shower of dry mortar and dust rained down upon the decorator. We stuck a holly branch through each hook hanging from the ceiling where they shared places with bits of "yalla" bacon. Behind the pictures was also a good holding place, and along the top of the kitchen press. Nobody called a halt to our free-flowing design and we did not consider the job finished until every scrap of holly had found a home. My grandmother had told us that an angel sat on top of every holly spike during the twelve days of Christmas, so we were determined to provide ample seating accommodation for visiting angels!

THE NIGHT BEFORE CHRISTMAS

We rushed through putting up the holly, but we took our time with decorating the Christmas tree. In our large farmhouse kitchen, around which the whole life of the house and farm revolved, were two timber tables which had to be scrubbed white every Saturday. The largest of the two was for family meals and the second acted as a stand for buckets of spring water and milk, but over Christmas these buckets found another stand and the table became the home of the Christmas tree. To describe ours as a tree was a bit of an exaggeration because it was actually a branch that my father, under pressure, cut for us. If he had been compelled actually to cut down one of his much loved trees, it would have turned us into Christmas orphans overnight. But he did usually concede a fine big pine branch, and this we placed on top of the table in a bucket of sand, where it stretched its dark green arms along the yellow walls; its main stem reached up beside the clock, whose brass pendulum swung back and forth behind the branches.

The decorations consisted of balloons and the Christmas cards that had come from relations all over the world during the previous weeks, together with the pick of the best of previous years. There was a long debate as to whose favourite card should enjoy pride of place at the top, but whoever won the argument knew that their victory was short-lived as whatever card headed the pole would be quietly replaced several times during the following days, and often indeed within the hour. As the decorating fervour swept us along, we sang and we argued, and occasionally a stand-up fight brought proceedings to a halt until my mother stepped in to restore the peace. A serene person herself, she was forever telling us that a row never solved a problem, only made it worse, but her advice mainly fell on deaf ears.

She brought the box containing the ceiling decorations out of the money trunk upstairs and we draped these long paper chains across the kitchen, attaching them to the ceiling with little tacks which we poked out of my father's butter box. The ceiling was fairly low, so we could not let them dip down too far: after all, Uncle Andy was over six feet tall, so they could finish up like a halo around his head or tangled in my father's cap. The partition around by the walls had a little shelf running along the top and here we ran the ivy; with the left-overs we draped the banister of the stairs. Despite our many arguments and power struggles we still hugely enjoyed smothering the kitchen with Christmas decorations and making it look totally different from its appearance during the rest of the year. At an enforced break for a makeshift meal we ate mashed potatoes from my mother's stuffing pot and ling with a white sauce. I hated the look of the ling and the smell of it, but because I was hungry and there was no alternative, I swallowed it, though I kept my eyes closed.

After we had all been fed my mother turned her attention to the stuffing. The steaming potatoes were allowed to cool slightly before peeling but could not be allowed to cool too much as they needed enough warmth to melt the big lump of yellow butter that streamed over them as they were put into a big green enamel dish that she always used for the stuffing. A large stale loaf had its insides slowly grated out with a fork and was blended through the potatoes together with sliced onions and her chosen herbs and spices. When it was all to her satisfaction she lined up the now pure white, washed and scrubbed goose beside the dish and slowly packed the stuffing in. As all the goose's departments were filled up she took on a new appearance and it was easy to forget that she had once been a grass goose before being fattened up for this end as our prospective dinner. When she was packed to capacity she was stitched up front and back and the spare stuffing was put into a bowl and covered with greaseproof paper. She was then laid in state in the green dish with the bowl on her stuffed belly and carried to the chilly regions of the lower room to wait for Christmas morning. The ham had been lifted out of the pot of boiling water and transferred to the bastable over the fire where it slowly roasted and filled the kitchen with a tempting smell. But Christmas Eve was a meatless day – "a hungry day" as Dan called it – so there was no hope of a tasting session later on.

With the goose out of the way, my mother turned her attention to the Christmas candle. There was no argument involved here because this was my mother's domain and we all bowed to her right to do it her way, following her instructions without question. My father brought in the big yellow turnip with an odd purple bulge which he had lifted from the turnip pit and scrubbed in the water barrel on his way in. He put it, still dripping, on the deep window-sill and proceeded to scoop out a hole with his penknife. He fitted and refitted the big white two-pound Christmas candle until it was rock-solid in position, making sure that it couldn't be overturned by his noisy brood whom he always considered capable of burning him out of house and home. With the candle standing pale and upright in its yellow bed, my mother wrapped a red, pleated paper skirt around the turnip. We had made the skirt the night before with crêpe paper and straight pins and with much ripping and patching. Now my mother stuck the best of the red-berry holly into the turnip, where it curved upwards around the candle and fell out over the frilled skirt. The dark green holly and the bright red berries

contrasted vividly with the tall white candle. Then she put holly all around the window-sill and shutters. We stood back, silenced by her serenity, and were impressed by the lovely effect she could achieve with the minimum of fuss.

Then she brought what she called her "Christmas mottoes", brightly coloured, unframed pictures, and hung them in their usual places. One depicted a fat Santa with an overflowing bag of toys and she placed it above the new oilcloth over the fireplace; another, of Mary and Joseph and the donkey, she put on the wall beside the oil lamp. Finally she positioned a little battered cardboard crib under the tree, and now we were ready for Santa.

We waited for our old neighbour Bill to come down from his hilltop house to inspect our efforts and when he did we formed a guard of honour around him as he inspected our Christmas layout. Then my brother staggered in the door under the weight of the Christmas log. My mother whipped the bastable containing the ham off the pot hangers and we ran to the fireplace ahead of him and scooped the fire forward with the big iron tongs and shovel to make way for the log so that it would fit snugly up against the red bricks at the back. He rocked it back and forth until it reached ground level and there was nothing large beneath it to upset its balance. It was just the right length and the same height as the red bricks behind the grate and was thick enough to back the fire for days. Along the front of it we laid long black sods of turf and slowly the disturbed fire recovered itself and flames licked out between the sods and up the front of the log where the dry moss and green lichen crackled and curled and revealed the solid white trunk beneath. The care taken in choosing "Blockeen na Nollag" had been worth while.

Then Bill sat with us beside the fire as we listened to Santa on the radio calling out in his rich, gravelly voice the names of all the boys and girls whom he was going to visit later that night. He was a wise Santa, because he called out long lists of Christian names only, so that somewhere along the line most children were included. When I heard my name called out I had no thought for any other Alice out there: that was my name he called out and later that night he was going to come down our chimney. When he had finished his lists and he announced that he was on his way from the North Pole, we went to the kitchen door and looked out over the distant Kerry hills; there in the fading light of the evening sky I was sure that I could see his sleigh in the gathering darkness on the horizon.

Our Christmas Visitor

WHEN DAN MADE his hasty departure after the threshing, having provoked a row with Bill, he told my father: "Boss, I'll be back for Christmas if I'm not dead or in jail. I'll have a roof over my head in either of those two place, but if they don't work out I'll be back." He never stayed with us very long because he soon got restless and wanted to be on the move. But he did not go quietly, because he did nothing quietly, so he provoked a row with anyone who was available and then he went off in a huff after demanding a clean shirt off my mother. She worried about him in case he did not look after himself properly and when he came to stay she always tried to fatten him up, but Nell told her she was wasting her time.

"No fat," Nell said, "would rest on that fella: he is too full of venom, it melts the fat off him." There was no love lost between himself and Nell.

But Dan and my mother got on well, even though they were a total contrast; she was easygoing and at peace with herself while Dan was like thorny wire and would fight with himself if there was no one else available. One day in a moment of appreciation he told her: "Missus, to live in this house you'd want to be a saint," and then – because there was always a sting in the tail where Dan was concerned – he added: "but then there is very little difference between a saint and a fool." Despite this pronouncement she always defended him when he succeeded in antagonising everybody else in the house.

That Christmas night Bill pointed out to us the different heavenly bodies in the night sky and we all stood looking up, trying to see if there was a very bright star up there that could be the star of Christmas. As we stood gazing up in a circle around Bill we heard a rasping cough and Dan's rough voice came out of the semi-darkness, cutting into our silent world.

"What the hell are ye all doing out here, standing looking up to heaven like fools?" he demanded, and without giving us a chance to answer he continued in a voice loaded with sarcasm: "Bill, are you thinking of ascending? You've the wrong season you know. This is Christmas, not Easter."

"How are you, Dan," Bill greeted him, ignoring the gibe. "You're here for Christmas."

"What do you think I'm here for: saving the hay?" Dan asked.

Suddenly Dan's Prince went tearing up the yard and got clung in a tangle with a few of our dogs. "Come back here, you fool!" Dan called. "Would you ever learn to size up the opposition before you attack?"

"Who do you suppose he's taking after?" Bill asked innocently.

But before Dan could answer I broke in with the good news: "Dan, Dan!" I shouted. "Prince is a father. Nell's Shep is after having his pups."

"Be the holy hoor," Dan said, "isn't he the miracle worker?"

"Nell is very annoyed about it," I told him primly.

Dan threw back his head and roared laughing: "Yerra, the ould bitch," he said; "no harm to give her a bit of a rattle!"

"You're full of the spirit of Christmas," Bill told him.

"Yerra, Christmas, me bum," Dan declared.

"Nell doesn't like Christmas either," I told him.

"Pity to be wasting two houses with ye," Bill told him; "you should move in with her for Christmas and the two of ye could mind the pups together."

"How would you like a broken nose for Christmas?" Dan demanded, shoving his fists into Dan's face. Bill was over six feet tall and about sixteen stone in weight, whereas Dan was not much more than five feet tall and was as thin as a sparrow. He looked like an aggressive terrier attacking a tranquil Great Dane. We all surrounded Bill and pushed Dan away, and just then my father appeared around the corner of the house.

"Well, Dan," he said, "the grave or jail didn't get you."

"No," Dan said, "so I had no choice but to come here, and I'm beginning to regret it already."

"Are they after upsetting you?" my father asked sympathetically, much to our annoyance. Dan was the cause of all the trouble as usual, but my father was very fond of him even though he was contrary and cranky.

"Between Father Christmas here," Dan said, pointing to Bill, "and all these children, I'll be deranged before Christmas is even started."

"Come on in and warm yourself to the fire. We'll be having the supper soon," my father told him, and they both disappeared into the kitchen. Though he was as edgy as a holly spike, we were still glad that Dan had come, because – like the holly spike – he was part of our Christmas.

When Dan and my father had gone into the kitchen, Bill and ourselves resumed our study of the night sky. It was a clear, bright night and the magic of Christmas was out there in the quiet countryside under the stars. Then we conveyed Bill homewards: down the yard, through the grove and "back over the ditch", as we called it, and then I sat there and waited for Johnny the Post.

Christmas Cards

JOHNNY WAS LATE that day, but then he was always late on Christmas Eve. I sat on the stony ditch behind the house waiting for the first glimpse of his navy cap through the darkness as he came across the fields. Sticking out between the stones of the ditch was an iron step. Originally it had been the step of an old back-to-back trap and my grandfather had buried it in between the stones as he had built the ditch. It provided a firm foothold and an adequate seat, and as it was sheltered by overhanging trees it was umbrella-dry.

As I sat there I watched shapes of the trees in the old fort behind the house standing motionless above the rattling glaise at their feet. They were like tall, dark shadows waiting quietly. Maybe, I thought, they were waiting for the snow, and I hoped that their wait would not be in vain because I wanted the snow to fill up the quiet valley and turn the countryside into a sparkling fairy-land.

Meanwhile I waited for Johnny: he would come up the glen from the next farmhouse, but the last light had faded so I could not see that far. A light film of frost lay like a white eiderdown on the blackthorn hedge along the boundary ditch. I knew that Johnny would soon come through a gap in that hedge bringing the last of the Christmas cards.

The first card had arrived very early in December, even before we had got our holidays from school. It had come all the way from New York in a big envelope with an airmail sticker and brightly coloured stamps. My father had met Johnny out in the fields. Half-way through his supper that night, he had pulled the card out of his pocket.

"Must be from Kate," he said dismissively, throwing the card on to the middle of the table; "no one else would be crazy enough to be sending Christmas cards and the threshing hardly over."

Sometimes my father had no sense of occasion, but if he did not, we made up for his inadequacies. We pounced on the envelope and, as we scrambled for possession, my mother had to intervene to decide who would have the thrill of opening Aunty Kate's card. I got the honour because I had a hold of it at the time.

I laid the large envelope on the table to flatten out the curve that my father's pocket had created. As my hand smoothed out the bump, I felt the stiff card inside resist the pressure: this was no light, flimsy card but a fine substantial model – a bit like Aunt Kate herself, I thought. The card within the envelope refused to be straightened out, so I peeled open the curved, gummed front carefully in order to avoid damage to its contents. It was certainly worth minding, and when I finally drew out the big red Santa card, we all gasped in appreciation.

As I eased him out of his narrow enclosure, the frost on the front of his large pot belly created a rough scratching sound against the envelope. Some of his glitter transferred itself on to my fingertips and I waved them about, fascinated by the sparkle. He was a beauty and when he stood in the middle of our kitchen table he brought the warmth and colour of Aunt Kate into her old home. She did not come home very often but when she did she made up for lost time and brought us big boxes of brightly coloured flimsy American clothes and filled the house with her perfume and laughter. She never wrote during the year but always at Christmas her big colourful card was the first to arrive and inside it were pages and pages of a letter in her sprawling, flamboyant writing. She was our favourite aunt and her Christmas card was the yearly connection that bound her to us.

After Aunty Kate's card there was a lull for a while, so every day we took out her Santa and admired him; it offered reassurance that Christmas was really coming. Next to arrive were calendars of St Francis and Blessed Martin with an assortment of holy pictures, and though they were better than nothing they were not quite the real thing and so generated no great excitement. These came from Br Matthew, a nephew of my father's, who was a Franciscian friar and visited us every summer. From inside his long flowing habit he would produce holy pictures, medals and rosary beads and sometimes sweets as well. He was a smiling, happy man and I sometimes thought that his flowing robes were like a folding cupboard they contained so much.

Then a card arrived from a cousin of my father's in London. He was in the police and his card was an etching of a dull, grey building and was briefly signed: "With best wishes – Doris and Jim". Nobody called Doris lived in our part of the country and I had only ever heard the name on the BBC. So, looking at her Christmas card, I tried to imagine what Doris looked like. Hopefully she was not as grey and dull as her card, but then maybe it was our cousin Jim who had chosen it, though if he was anything like my father that was highly unlikely.

My mother bought the Christmas cards for my father's relations as well as her own. She bought them with great care and she went to lot of trouble to find verses suitable for the recipients. But when she sent a verse advocating joyous festive feelings to an old aunt whose list of ailments provided her greatest interest in life, I thought that she was overestimating the power of the spirit of Christmas.

Into most of her cards she put a letter. She spent many nights in the weeks before the festive season writing them by the light of the oil lamp at the kitchen table, often into the small hours of the morning. At that time of year she remembered in particular the family members of the previous generation who had left our house to go to destinations all over the world. She felt that, as the woman who had married into the family farm, it was up to her to send them greetings from their old home. She always spoke about "the people away" and how important it was to remember them and to keep in contact. She knew from listening to some of them when they came on summer holidays that at Christmas their thoughts turned to home and they loved to be remembered at that time. For others the card was even more important; it provided the only link they had because they never made it home. I visualised my mother's Christmas cards as so many messengers winging their way to scattered family members all over the world from the nest from which they or their parents had all flown. She was the warm glow at the heart of our Christmas, but that warmth stretched much further than our house.

Sometimes one of her Christmas correspondents might miss a Christmas, and then she would wonder if everything was all right with them and would be delighted when the card arrived the following year. But she never failed to send her cards every year, as she maintained that the people away needed them more than the ones at home.

As we drew closer to Christmas the bundle of cards

that Johnny drew out of his bag grew bulkier and each of us was eager to be the one to meet him. He was a small, thin cherry-faced man and his large mailbag stretched from beneath his arm to just above his knee. When he turned his head sideways to peer into its interesting depths, he somehow reminded me of one of our hens tucking her head under her wing to go to sleep. But sleep was the last thing on Johnny's mind and he had his letters very well organised, whipping them out of his bag and waving them above our heads so that we had to jump up to get them.

As the Christmas mail grew heavier, Johnny's day grew longer until on Christmas Eve it was dark before he reached our house. By then we had received most of our cards and they were strung up around the house and hanging off the Christmas tree. As the list of Christmas card senders scarcely varied from year to year, I knew who remained outstanding and among them was Uncle Dan in Oregon, who every year sent a big card with robins or reindeers. Next to Aunt Kate's his was the best Christmas card, but whereas she was always early he was always late and I worried in case his did not make it in time. Without Uncle Dan's card on top of the tree beside Aunt Kate's, Christmas would not seem quite right.

So I waited for Johnny and thought of Uncle Dan, who had left this house as a young lad of eighteen to go sheep farming in Oregon and who had never come back. Every Christmas my mother wrote to him telling him all the news and every Christmas he sent his lovely card. In a strange way as long as his card was on the tree he was in some way there for Christmas. It was the one card that my father loved to get, and when it arrived he smiled and I knew then that he was ready to enjoy Christmas.

At last a black shadow that turned out to be Johnny

came through the muddy gap beside the fort. As he drew near I could see that the Christmas spirit that people had given him to celebrate the season of good will had gone slightly to Johnny's head and his balance was not what it should have been. Despite this he had our bundle ready. As I followed him into the kitchen, I pulled the hairy twine from around the cards. I sighed with relief when I saw the big envelope with the American stamp: Uncle Dan had made it in time. But Johnny had a surprise in his bag: much to our amazement he put in his hand and pulled out a parcel. Very seldom did we get a parcel of any description, and when we did it was the cause of great excitement even if it was only a sample of flies for my father's fishing rod. But a parcel on Christmas Eve could only mean one thing – a present! However, we never received Christmas presents through the post. Santy certainly came, but presents wrapped up in parcels were unheard of. Now we stood around Johnny with our mouths open.

"Don't ye want it?" he asked, pretending to put it back in his bag. Four pairs of hands shot up to grab it off him, but he handed it over our heads to my mother and disappeared out the door. It was a sign of how flabbergasted my mother was that she left him go without offering him tea.

"Will I open it?" she asked of no one in particular.

"Yerra don't bother," my father told her; "sure, no one is interested in what's in it anyway."

His caustic comment brought her to her senses and she looked down at all the curious faces peering intently at her. She took the parcel over to the kitchen table and placed it carefully in the centre. We all stood around looking at it.

"Well," my father enquired, "will we open it or will we have a guessing game as to what's inside?"

"I wonder who sent it," my mother said, mystified.

"If someone opened it we'd find out," my father told her.

"Could it be Kate I wonder?" My mother was talking to herself rather than to us.

"'Twould be like something she'd do," my father said in a tone of voice which implied that she was capable of anything.

At this stage we were all getting restless and were starting to poke and prod at the parcel to ascertain what it might contain. It was quite hard so I decided that there must be a tin box inside the paper wrapping.

"Would you open the damn thing before they have it torn asunder," my father advised my mother.

Carefully she peeled back the paper, taking pains not to tear the stamps. We were restless with anticipation and her slow and careful opening of the parcel had us dancing with impatience around the table. At last the paper was removed to reveal a red box that did not seem to have an opening, and as my mother's fingers searched around to solve the problem she must have touched a spring, for suddenly the top shot up and a small man popped out. He had a yellow hat, a black face and a red jacket over a white shirt and black dickie bow and he danced up and down in delight at being released.

"A jack-in-the-box!" we all exclaimed in delight.

"Just what we need," my father declared, "and I having six already." He was forever telling us to sit still and not to be like jack-in-the-box, and because we had never seen one Aunty Kate had decided to send us a real one. We were delighted.

"No one but Kate would send such a daft thing halfway across the world," my father said, shaking his head. Later, when I looked up at their cards on the

Christmas tree and thought of Uncle Dan out under the stars on the prairies of Oregon and Aunty Kate in New York, I felt that in some way they were with us that night.

The Night Before Christmas

THE LIGHTING OF the Christmas candle marked the transition from day into night on Christmas Eve. But before that could be done the farmyard had to be closed down. My father went to the barn and tied a rope around a bundle of hay, as much as he could carry. He hoisted it on to his back, staggering at first under the weight until he got his balance beneath it; then he jolted it upwards until it rested on the back of

his head and shoulders; he held it securely in place with the rope coming up over his shoulder and pulled down firmly in front of him by one hand and wound around the other. He walked slowly beneath his awkward load, balancing each foot carefully, his heavy nailed boots clattering off the stone haggard. He gathered speed when he reached the field with the soft sod underfoot and the hill to his back. Watching him walk down the fields in the dusk of the evening, he looked like a walking cock of hay as all you could see were his gaitered legs beneath the load. The sheep, huddled under the hedge in the lower meadow, bleated a welcome to him. They were the only farm animals who would spend Christmas out in the fields; just like the sheep on the first Christmas, they too were out under the stars that were now starting to glitter in the darkening sky.

Our job was to lock up the hens, who were nestled high on the perches of the hen-house; some had already retired for the night with their heads under their wings. We shot the bolt on the galvanised door in case Mr Fox came during the night in search of an early Christmas dinner. Only the gander and his mother goose gossiped together in the rusty roofed shed in the corner of the haggard. Their year's work was done and they were relaxing before the cycle began again. Together with all the other animals, they were resting. In the stalls some of the cows chewed the cud while others had strings of hay dribbling from their soft mouths, their large, moist eyes staring placidly into space. The stalls were full of their damp bovine smell and their body heat had taken the chill out of the cold night air. From them there was no reaction when we opened the door and walked in amongst them; only a few turned big trusting eyes in our direction. But the horses were all movement and questioning looks when we opened the stable door. Their curious heads curved back towards us and their hind legs stamped on the cobbled floor. Cobwebs draped off the high rafters above their heads and their tackling hung off the wall behind them and in here the smell was of horse sweat and leather. In the stable was one empty manger and in my imagination it was to this manger later that night that Mary and Joseph would come and the baby would be born. It did not have a donkey, but the jennet was the next best thing, though I was glad that he was tied up because no baby would be safe beside him.

As we returned to the house the moon was coming up over the Kerry mountains on the horizon, rising into a dark-blue sky. Down by the river we could dimly see the sheep in the corner of the field. When we passed the kitchen window the dancing flames from the blazing fire outshone the soft yellow glow of the oil lamp. We were glad to get in from the cold and stand with our backs to the fire, our long skirts pulled up so that we could warm our cold bottoms.

We laid the table with great care because tonight we were going to have things on it which we had not seen since the previous Christmas, and this was the only occasion other than when we had visitors on which we used a table-cloth. It was a long white cloth with yellow edgings which my mother had got as a wedding present from a favourite aunt. Frances had gone to a cookery night-class in town over the last few months and one of the results of her studies was an iced Christmas cake. She had arrived home with it the night before and we were speechless with admiration when we saw it. Now the cake took pride of place in the centre of the table surrounded by seed loaf – my father's favourite – barm brack and swiss roll. The anticipation on looking at them all laid out on the table was enough to tempt preliminary sampling but this was strictly forbidden by the cake-maker. My brother was the self-appointed maker of toast, which he always decided should be part of the Christmas supper. The glowing red fire turned the bread golden brown. He buttered it generously as he went along and the smell of toast filled the kitchen. When two stacks of toast running over with butter propped each other up in the big dish before the fire, we were ready for the supper. But first the candle had to be lit. In my mother's world the needs of the stomach were secondary to the rituals and spirituality of the season. Nothing could to be eaten until the candle had been lit.

My father always had matches in his pocket to light his pipe and it was his job to light the candle. We gathered in a semi-circle around the window where the candle rested on the deep sill. The world outside was dark,

and when my father cracked a match the flame was reflected in the window pane. When he put it to the candle, at first the wick spluttered and blackened but then it slowly reddened and a yellow flame kindled and rose upwards. Its reflection glowed in the window and another family looked in at us.

My mother had the bottle of holy water ready and she sprinkled us liberally, which brought a protest from my father: "Len, are you trying to bless us or drown us?"

I licked up the salty spatter of holy water that had landed on my chin and watched the first tiny stream of candle grease run down on to the holly. The lighted candle was the symbol that Christmas was finally here. The magic of Christmas was out in the moonlit haggard with the cattle and down the fields with the sheep, but most of all it was here in the holly-filled kitchen with the little battered crib under the tree and the tall candle lighting in the window. The candle was the light of Christmas and the key that opened the door into the holy night.

Then we gathered around the table and as we tucked in we were like our geese in the haggard after the threshing. The first onslaught over, my mother decided to cut the Christmas cake. She had on a new bib which she very aptly termed her "coat-overall" and the starched cotton folds crackled as she rose to bend over the cake. The hard icing resisted her efforts and my father asked, much to my sister's annoyance, "Will we bring in the sledge?" But soon the first dark cut emerged and we discovered that heavy fruit cake was not to be scoffed with the same abandon as the other cakes. At last we were all creaking at the seams. My father withdrew to his seat by the fire and we washed up the ware in a tin pan on the corner of the table. One of us washed, another dried and the third stacked them back into the kitchen press. We made no delay because we wanted to bring the gramophone down out of the parlour and the time to do this was when we had cleared away after the supper. Then my brother went to town for confession. We had gone the previous Saturday but he considered himself too big to go with the children.

The place for the gramophone was up on the corner of the table that held the Christmas tree, and as soon as it was in position we started to play our new records, my father warning us not to wind it too tightly and break the spring. If that happened we would be in right trouble because it would mean the bleak prospect of a Christmas without the gramophone. All the records got trial runs, and as the night progressed a favourite emerged in the form of "Come Back, Paddy Reilly, to Ballyjamesduff".

THE NIGHT BEFORE CHRISTMAS

My mother once told me that when I was born,
The day that I first saw the light,
I looked down the street on that very first morn,
And gave a great crow of delight.
Now most new born babies appear in a huff,
And start with a sorrowful squall,
But I knew I was born in Ballyjamesduff,
And that's why I smiled at them all.
The baby's a man, now he's toil-worn and tough,
Still, whispers come over the sea,
"Come back, Paddy Reilly, to Ballyjamesduff,
"Come home, Paddy Reilly, to me".

This was played constantly until my father began to
regret that his mother had not drowned Paddy Reilly in
his baby bath water; even my mother decided that her
eardrums needed a break and suggested lemonade and
biscuits. It was only at Christmas that we had this

treat, so we lined up eagerly as my father forced the tin tops off with the bottle opener; then we sat around the fire sipping and slugging out of the bottles and helping ourselves from the plate of biscuits on the table. My father, Uncle Andy and Dan drank porter, which my mother poured into glasses with sugar; then my father plunged a hot poker into the cold black porter and it frothed up and ran down the sides of the glasses. It smelt gorgeous, and when my mother was not looking Uncle Andy gave me a sip, but it tasted horrid and I was glad to go back to my lemonade.

My brother arrived home as we were having our lemonade and he had a brown parcel under his arm which immediately started an inquisition. He held us in suspense for a long time, baiting our curiosity, but in the end he took off the brown paper and inside was a box of chocolates. What a box of chocolates! It was the first to find its way into our house. Long, sleek and golden with the name written in darker gold writing. It spelt out Urney, and when I ran my fingers over the letters they were slightly raised and felt like velvet. We smelt it and we felt it. It was something from another world!

The explanation of how he had got this unaccustomed luxury delighted my mother much more than the box itself.

"Arthur O'Keeffe is home from America: I met him in town," he told her. She was delighted and it seemed to add to the charm of the box that her cousin Arthur was home and had bought it for us. We children did not care where it had come from, only that it was here and waiting to be opened. As my brother was the recipient, he got the honour of doing the opening. When he eased off the outer wrapper the box beneath was a replica, and when he lifted up the cover there was dark brown glossy paper covering the hidden treasure. When this was turned back a soft white pad appeared with gold lettering and beneath, in sunken sections, lay rows and rows of chocolates, some wearing gold and silver wrappings. When we had satisfied our visual senses it was time to taste; they looked so perfect that I felt it was a shame to take one out, but still my mouth was watering in anticipation. The white pad which told the story of each chocolate was consulted before decisions were made. My choice was big and smooth in my mouth and then it melted slowly and its coffee contents poured out over my tongue: it was gorgeous! After the first free round they were rationed and the box placed on top of the radio in full view of everybody, so that even distribution would be guaranteed at regular intervals.

My mother hung the kettle over the fire and brought a big red glass bowl from the parlour and placed it on the kitchen table, where she lined it with the left-over swiss roll and broken biscuits. We tore up squares of red jelly, dropping them into a white enamel jug; when the kettle was steaming my mother poured the boiling water over the jelly and we took our turns at swirling it around in the hot water until it melted; then my mother poured it into the red bowl where the swiss roll and biscuits soaked it up.

My father lit the storm lantern and went out to see the cows and when he came back in he sat in front of the fire and slowly unlaced his heavy leather boots. Sometimes he paused and gazed into the fire and I sensed that his thoughts were of other Christmas nights and the people who were gone with them. He did not say anything, but after my chat with Mrs Casey I knew that Christmas held many memories for him. Then it was time to say the rosary, and as my father slid to his knees and rested his elbows on the *súgán*

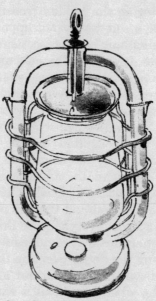

chair, I sensed that he was glad of this period of quiet reflection. I knelt inside the candle-lit window and out there I saw Mary and Joseph on their way to the stable.

Once the rosary was over my father, after winding the clock, headed for bed, telling us as he went that if Santa came by and we were still up he would keep going. Faced with this terrible possibility we sat on the warm flagstone before the fire and unlaced our boots and eased off our long black stockings. The fire had burnt low in front of the Christmas log, which crackled gently, sighed and sent a soft white smoke drifting up the chimney. I looked up after the smoke and imagined that I could see a red boot coming down. As we put our stockings across the crane, the certainty that later that night while we were sound asleep upstairs the wonderful figure of Santa would actually come down this chimney and step from the crane on to the spot where we were now standing was a thrilling prospect. The stockings were arranged and rearranged until finally my mother gently intervened and advised on the best layout; as they all hung there they presented a picture of great expectations.

Then, bearing a candle and sconce, we went upstairs to bed.

Christmas

BECAUSE IT WAS cold that night, my mother lit a fire in the small iron grate beneath the white mantelpiece in the bedroom. We sat on the floor around it in our long flannelette night-dresses, our bare feet lined along the top of the black fender, warming our toes and wondering if Santa would make a detour off the main chimney and peep in at us on his way down to the kitchen, where our stockings were hanging off the black crane over the fire.

I had watched Black Ned sweep the chimney, so I knew that the way downward was clean and ready to welcome Santa when his sleigh parked on top of our roof. Ours was a real Santa Claus chimney: because it was wide he would have no difficulty in getting in at the top, and down along were iron brads to act as footholds. The only thing that worried me slightly was the fact that he might get some of the fresh soot on his lovely red suit, but I decided that Santa probably did not mind just a little bit of soot. Sitting on the bare, fawn mat in front of the fire, we watched imaginary pictures fade and reappear in the red sods of turf between the iron bars of the narrow grate. I saw the donkey with Our Lady on his back climbing a steep hill; the sods shifted, that picture disappeared and Santa sped into view, and then he was gone and I saw a full stocking hanging off a crane. We took our turns describing what we had seen. The fine turf ashes beneath the high grate glowed and with the long poker we drew sketches of Santa on his way across the sky to us. Our minds were full of the wonder that during this very night his mysterious figure was going to be really here in our own house.

A candle in a white enamel sconce sat on the mantelpiece above us and joined the firelight in casting shadows along the low timber ceiling. We were reluctant to leave the pool of warmth before the fire, to run across the icy-cold lino on the floor and into the still colder beds. But the thought that Santa might come and look in the window and pass on because we were not in bed forced our decision.

The last in the race to the two big iron beds under the sloping roof had to dash back and quench the candle. The top of the wick glowed red for a few seconds in the darkness and its smouldering smell and that of the hot candle-grease filled the room. The dying fire sighed in the grate and its orange glow was the only light in the pitch-blackness of the bedroom. We pulled the heavy quilts up under our chins and burrowed our bottoms and heels into the soft feather ticks, bouncing the spring bases up and down to keep ourselves warm.

Our whispered conversation gradually faded and I started to doze off with my eyes on the door in the far corner, thinking that Santa might come up from the kitchen just to peep in at us. Then I jerked myself awake and sat up to check on the fireplace, bringing a squeal of protest from my sister because I had let the cold in around her. But there was no Santa peering down the chimney. Then through the black bars of the iron bed I watched the window in case he might look in that way. Despite my visual journey around the room, sleep got the better of me and I drifted off, thinking that Santa's face was smiling down at me between the twisted timber knots in the low ceiling.

When I awoke the room was full of darkness and absolute silence. I listened and tried to detect from the
breathing beside me and from the bed across the room
if anyone else was awake, but it was impossible to be
sure. I wondered if it was still the middle of the night,
but then from the hen-house in the yard the cock crew
loud and clear. It was morning.

"Anyone awake?" I whispered.

"I am," came a voice from the other side.

"Will we go down and see what he brought?"

The answer was a ghostly figure in a long white
night-dress rising out of the other bed and jumping on
to the floor with a thud. She felt her way along by the
wall and opened the door and the loose brass knob rattled and woke our other two sisters. We groped our way
in the darkness along the narrow landing, under the
skylight which glinted with grey frost and threw an
eerie light down the high, narrow stairs. We trouped
down silently, breathless with anticipation, and I was
glad of the comfortable warmth of the kitchen where
the Christmas log still glowed under the crane; it was a
welcome change from the chilly upstairs regions.

Bulging stockings hung off the crane and interesting
looking packets lay on the floor beside the bellows. We
forced the lumps out of the stockings, squealing with
delight as oranges, crayons and coloured pencils popped
forth. Then the packets on the floor yielded story books,
snakes-and-ladders, ludo, two jumpers and a new
school bag. I searched around through the discarded
stockings and papers, hoping that the doll that I had
written to Santa for was buried in the debris, but after
a few minutes I gave up hope. A stab of disappointment
shot through me: I had been so sure he would bring
one. But when I picked up my school sack and put my
nose deep into it to absorb the gorgeous smell of the

fresh leather, inside I discovered a little green cloth doll with black button eyes. He was soft and cuddly and I immediately christened him Patsy. Santa had not let me down after all!

We sat on the floor playing snakes-and-ladders and tried out the new crayons in the light of the Christmas candle, which had stood overnight in the big turnip in the window. As the hands of the eight-day clock on the wall moved on towards seven o'clock, two of us went reluctantly back upstairs to get ready to walk the three miles to eight o'clock Mass in the town.

We burst into our parents' room to show them what Santa had brought and were surprised that they were not more surprised by what we had got. My sister put on the new red jumper, which had a row of small white ducks across the front of it. I envied her a little but put Patsy into the pocket of my coat, and as my fingers curled around him, I decided that he was better than any row of white ducks.

When we opened the door we gasped as the cold early morning air hit us like an icy cloth across the face. The pathway out through the garden was covered with a hard black frost and our leather shoes clattered over the slippery stones. We peered in through the kitchen window at our sisters still playing on the floor inside. The red-berry holly glistened in the candlelight and a stream of candle-grease like a giant icicle had formed overnight on the turnip. Next year it would be the turn of our other two sisters to go to the early Mass and to come home to mind the goose that my mother would put into the bastable over the fire, to cook slowly while she was at Mass. The goose now sat in the green dish inside the window waiting for the next stage of her journey on to the Christmas table.

As we walked up the hilly, winding boreen that led from our farmhouse to the road, I was glad that we were out early on that Christmas morning. The stars sparkled high in a dark blue sky and Christmas candles saluted us from the windows of the houses on the hills that stretched away into the Kerry mountains. We were alone out there in that quiet countryside. The silence was impressive and we felt part of this solitary world. On an ordinary morning the hills would have been covered in a blanket of darkness, but Christmas morning was different because the candles lit up the hills and the valleys as far as we could see.

As we walked along we strained our ears for the sound of horse's hooves, which would mean a lift in a horse and trap to shorten the journey. But no sound broke the silence, and as we walked together we discussed the wonders of Santa and I held Patsy firmly in my pocket where no cold could touch him and my sister felt the ribbed edge of her new red jumper that peeped down the sleeves of her coat. No one in the world was as wonderful as Santa that morning and as we walked along we stopped when we reached gaps in the ditches to look across the moonlit countryside to see if he was still doing his rounds.

When we arrived in town the streets were deserted, but as we walked up the steep hill to the church we were joined by people hurrying in the same direction. After the darkness outside we blinked in the blaze of light inside, and the high white marble altar, which normally looked cold and remote, was bright and festive with red-berry holly. From the choir high up in the gallery came waves of exuberant Christmas carols, while peals of organ music vibrated off the arching rafters. I knew very few of the carols but still loved to listen, joining in with the bits that I did know. Fr Roche, our grey-haired parish priest, wished us all a happy Christmas and welcomed home the emigrants, whom I recognised easily because they were more smartly dressed than the rest of us.

There was a long line for communion, including ourselves, and we had been fasting since before midnight. I became restless waiting for Mass to be over because I wanted to visit the crib. Deep in my pocket I had two big brown pennies to drop into the timber box. When Mass was finally over we made our way down the red quarry-tiled church to the stable sheltered in the corner under the gallery steps. We peered in over the golden straw at the donkey and cow at the back with the shepherds, and at Our Lady and St Joseph. I felt a bit sorry for St Joseph because he looked frail and bald and I thought that he was maybe a bit too old for his new responsibility. Our Lady was young and beautiful and I hoped that she would be kind to Joseph. But it was the

baby we both wanted to see. There he lay with outstretched arms, smiling up at us, and I thought that
Our Lady should have more clothes on him as the
morning was so cold. But he looked as happy as I felt. I
closed my eyes and wished him "Happy Birthday" and
dropped his present of my two big brown pennies into
his box.

When we came out of the church a grey morning had
replaced the darkness. As we made our way through
the silent town, the cold numbed our fingers and toes,
but as we climbed the hilly road homewards our toes
soon warmed up. We looked in through the iron farm
gates at the grey-white fields that were deserted of animals but for the sheep that were huddled into shady
corners. As we walked along we watched our breath
curl upwards in the cold air and blew into our knitted
gloves to keep our fingers warm.

Before she left for second Mass, my mother issued
more instructions than a departing general leaving an
inadequate army in charge of operations. She was torn
between the need for the goose to be basted and the
possibility that we might scald ourselves or even turn
the bastable upside down. So she decided to play safe
and let the goose take her chances; she finally departed
giving strict instructions not to leave the fire go down
but not to create an inferno, and to change the hot
griosach, or sods, around the top of the bastable at least
once during her absence. My father at this stage was
frothing at the mouth, so she was compelled eventually
to leave her precious goose in our care.

When we had the kitchen to ourselves, our first prior-
ity was to settle down to attack the big baked ham in
the centre of the table. This was the ham that had ma-
tured up the chimney and hung off the meat hook from
the ceiling; my mother had boiled and baked it in a

shroud of breadcrumbs and honey, and now all her loving care paid dividends because it was beautifully moist and tender. We always had ham for our breakfast on Christmas morning and it did nothing to lessen our appreciation of it when it reappeared again with the goose. Gradually the goose made her presence felt when she started to sizzle and splutter in the bastable and filled the kitchen with a smell that promised great things later on. When we had the ware washed and the kitchen tidied up, we very carefully brought the pots of potatoes and turnips from the lower room to beside the fire. We gripped the heavy black pots firmly by the ears, balancing the weight between us, and when we had settled them by the fire we changed the hot sods on the cover over the goose. Deciding that we had now discharged our responsibilities, we turned our attention to the gramophone; with the majority absent we had free

choice of records, so we were determined to take advantage of the situation. I loved the kitchen at this stage
because it was scattered with the generosity of Santa
and filled with a mixture of smells full of hidden
promises.

When my mother arrived home, she resumed control
of operations. The bastable with the goose inside was
moved sideways and the potatoes took centre stage,
then the turnips, and gradually by a process of skill-
fully swinging long black pot hangers into strategic positions around the fire all the pots came to boiling point
and got simmering time. The cover of the bastable was
removed a few times to baste the goose; removing the
cover was an exercise in balance and toleration of heat.
My mother got the long iron tongs and lifted the hot
griosach off the cover and then, taking a very firm grip
of the tongs, she eased the nose of it in under the handle in the centre of the cover. The aim then was to hold
the heavy cover in perfect balance or otherwise the hot
ashes that were still on the cover could tilt sideways in
on top of the goose. When she had the cover clear of the
bastable she would place it down very carefully on the
stone hearth and then she would spoon the hot well of
fat from around the goose down over her breast. Then
she slowly replaced the cover and restored the hot
griosach. When she judged that things were drawing to
a conclusion, she dispatched one of us with a jug and
spoon to take the cream off a bucket of milk that was
standing in the chilly quarters of the lower room; this
would afterwards be poured over the trifle that we had
made the night before.

Finally the moment arrived when the goose was
ready to emerge and we all gathered around to witness
her debut. My mother swung the bastable off the crane
and landed it on the hearth and then she lifted down

the big brown dish off the top shelf of the ware press and placed it on the floor beside the bastable. She lifted the cover off very slowly because a shower of ashes was the last thing my mother wanted over our goose at that point. We looked down at the bird where she sat, golden brown surrounded by slightly singed butter papers and stuffing overflowing from her front and rear quarters. She was transferred carefully into the dish where stuffing oozing butter settled in around her and her rich aromatic smell rose to the ceiling and curled downwards to fill the kitchen. While she rested on the table my mother made the gravy with the remains in the oven and the juice of the giblets; when she poured it, rich and thick, over our piled plates my misgivings of the previous night were long forgotten. The stuffing from inside the goose was excavated like hidden treasure and, when that source was exhausted, my mother removed the browned greaseproof paper from the top of the earthenware bowl that held the reserves. This stuffing was not as moist or as butter-laden as the other and we rated it as a lesser grade. We had never heard of cholesterol or the virtues of a fat-free diet!

By the time we had finished with the goose she was all legs and bony breast and it was we who were stuffed. But we still had room for the trifle and cream, and as we licked the plates the Queen's speech was beginning on the BBC. My father insisted on absolute silence as we listened. I loved her posh accent but felt sorry for her that she had to make a speech while we were all free to have our dinner.

Nobody wanted to do the washing up, but Frances hid the handle of the gramophone and refused to divulge its hiding place until the table was cleared, and that proved sufficient to motivate her reluctant work-force. Then we sat around the table playing snakes-and-lad-

ders and put record after record on the gramophone,
each taking it in turn to play their choice until finally
my father could no longer stand the racket and decided
that the cows needed to be checked. As the darkness
gathered in around the kitchen, we could no longer see
the numbers on the dice and decided that it was time to
light the lamp. When we looked out the window we discovered that while we had been engrossed in our game
it had started to snow. It was whirling down in big soft
flakes and the grove of trees below the house was disappearing beneath a white blanket. Because we lived in
a hilly region, the winters often brought snow, but it
never lost its wonder and the sight of it always filled us
with delight. Now my mother decided that it was too
late to go out, so we had to content ourselves with
watching it out through the window, occasionally running briefly out to the door to check on progress. When
my father came in from his trip down the fields to bring
hay to the sheep, he stamped his boots on the floor and
soft pads of packed snow fell on to the hearth and
melted in the heat of the fire.

After a supper of left-overs it did not take much per-
suasion to convince us that it was bedtime. We dragged
ourselves up the stairs, each one holding on to something brought that morning by Santa. I cuddled down
under the heavy quilt with Patsy on the pillow beside
me. Outside the window the snow was turning the fir
trees in the grove into real Christmas trees.

Hunting the Wren

W E AWOKE THAT morning to a white, silent world.
The light in the bedroom had a strange yel-
low-white hue from the reflected brightness of
the snow. Through the bedside window we could see the
trees in the grove outside: overnight they had been
transformed from a dark green military formation into
a still, white, pristine presence. Normally these trees
rustled and whispered among themselves and birds
were always on the move amongst them, but now there
was no movement. Beautiful but lifeless, they were
silent white statues and their snow-laden branches re-
sembled the outstretched arms of graceful ballerinas.
Not a bird was to be seen or heard.

"We'd better get up and feed the birds," Frances announced. But that morning all I wanted to do was to lie
there and look out through the window at the transformed world outside; however, I soon had the quilt
dragged off me and had no choice but to move. We
looked out the gable-end window and the sloping roof
on the lower part of the house lay spread out before us
like a pure white sheet. The front window looked out
over white fields which stretched down to the river valley; from there the land rose again and the farms on
the hill across the river faced us and the farmhouses
seemed to have shrunk in size beneath the snow; this
white land rolled away into distant hills and on the far
horizon we could see the white outline of the Kerry
mountains. The hedges on the hill across the river were

huddled under the snow and the sheep down in the river valley were the only sign of life in the whole scene. Contrasted with the brilliance of the snow, their colour had changed to yellow.

Then into our silent world came the sound of music coming down the boreen. The Wren Boys! We had forgotten about them with the excitement of the snow. We peered out the window, straining for a sight of them, but as yet the only sign of them was the music. It rolled over the silent farmyard and James, our old horse, gave a nervous neigh in the stable at this sudden intrusion of sound into his quiet corner. In the surrounding silence of the snow, the sound of the melodeon vibrated richly, filling the air with a charge of activity. No footsteps could be heard in the padded underfoot conditions, so we had only the music by which to judge their advance. As it grew louder we held our breath and then

they burst into the quiet yard where their outrageous
costumes contrasted vividly with the white background. There were about eight of them, dressed in all
kinds of odd-looking garments: tall, long-legged men
disguised in women's skirts and coats turned inside
out, and girls in their fathers' pants hitched up with
safety pins and bits of twine. They all had their faces
blackened or covered in cloths with cut-outs for the
mouth and eyes, and on their heads was an amazing
range of hats and caps. The leader carried the
melodeon and they trouped behind him as they ap-
proached the front door, laughing and jostling each
other. They started to chant:

The wran, the wran, the king of all birds,
St Stephen's Day was caught in the furze;
Up with the kettle and down with the pan
And give us some money to bury the wran.

We ran from the bedroom to the top of the stairs from
where we could watch them in action. They filed into
the kitchen, making sure that their faces were well
covered to preserve their disguise. The man with the
melodeon sat on a chair beside the stairs and the rest
of them lined up to dance a set to his music. They
bounced off the stone floor and at first the snow flew in
all directions from their boots and wellingtons. As they
whirled around we tried to guess who they were. We
had no problem in identifying one man who towered
over the rest and danced with his back poker-straight
and his knees almost hitting his jaw; Dan commented
loudly that he was like a gate-pillar in motion. Though
we realised that they must all be neighbours well
known to us, still it was difficult to put names on them.
As the music continued I watched the fingers flying up
and down the keys of the melodeon and realised that I
had watched those fingers many times and that they

belonged to our friend Martin, but there was no way I was going to let him know that I had recognised him. When the set was over, one of them sang a song in a disguised voice, which sent his companions into convulsions of laughter. As they filed out, the last to go held out a cap for any contribution that might be forthcoming. My mother gave each group of wren boys the same donation, but my father believed that the better the performance the bigger the reward.

After a hurried breakfast we got ourselves dressed up to go hunting the wren. It was the first year that I was considered old enough to survive a day on the wren trail and I was thrilled to bits to be taking part rather than just observing. Every year I had watched the wren boys come to our house and had wanted to join in the dressing up and the jaunt around the countryside. I got into my brother's pants and an old discarded coat of my father's and covered my face in an old tea towel with cut-out holes to avoid suffocation and donned my father's cap turned back to front. Now I felt that I had turned into another person. Everything was too big for me so sleeves were rolled up and trouser legs tied up with safety pins but the cap was a perfect fit when my long hair was tucked up under it.

There were five of us in the group: one sister and my brother, and two cousins who had arrived from town that morning to join us, and we were a motley-looking crew kitted out in clothes that were either too big or too small. Our only source of music was a mouth organ which none of us could play properly, but at least it gave us background music, and despite the fact that most of us knew very little about set-dancing we decided that it would be part of our entertainment. The only strong point we had in our repertoire was my brother's singing voice, and even though it would identify us, we felt that we had to capitalise on our one asset. My father had always asserted that wren boys should provide entertainment, so we felt that we should at least make a gallant effort. We decided that we would make a start with the dancing and finish with the song to leave a good parting impression, a bit like the wedding feast at Cana. We had the wind taken out of our sails in one house when the woman of the house announced to her husband that she had never seen dancing quite like ours before. A visitor from London, who was sitting by the fire, remarked that she considered it a bit tribal. It was not a great start, but things got better as we went on and in every house silence descended when my brother started to sing and we knew that we had them. I could see as we went along that he sang different songs in different houses and his choice was always right. In one house where there was an old couple, he sang "Silent Night" and I could see the old lady's face light up with delight.

"God bless you," she said; "that was beautiful."

By then we were miles from home and I no longer knew the people. "Who was she?" I asked him when we got outside.

"She taught in our school when I went there first and she taught us 'Silent Night'."

"But that must be a long time ago," I said in surprise.

"It is, but I never forgot her," he told me. "She was a real lady."

It was interesting to go into strange houses and to see the way they had decorated for Christmas, but one farmhouse provided a bit of a shock, for here there was neither tree nor decoration, only a bare candle in a jam-pot on the window. It could have been any ordinary day of the year and I felt very sorry for the children who stood around the kitchen. I had thought that Christmas was important in every house; to find that it was not frightened me a little.

"Why is there no Christmas in that house?" I asked my brother on leaving.

"You're all questions," he protested.

"But why?" I persisted.

"Because money is more important to them," he told me, and I sensed that that was all the information I was going to get. But the memory of that bare kitchen stayed with me for the rest of the day.

When we had started collecting in the morning, I had thought that this money was the softest we would ever earn, but as the day wore on I began to have second thoughts. My brother led us across endless fields until I lost all sense of direction. The deep snow slowed our progress, and when we clambered over ditches the snow came down on top of us and some of it found its way down the back of my neck. Jumping off ditches

where the snow had drifted against them, we sank deep
into it and the effort of continually pulling my legs out
of it was exhausting. Apart from the struggle with the
snow, my legs also had to contend with the extra burden of trying to set-dance and also to carry clothes that
were too large and too heavy. Hunting the wren was not
all plain sailing! But the hunger was the biggest problem, and I felt that my stomach and backbone were in
close contact. It was getting dark and I was beginning
to think that I would never again see home when one of
the town cousins produced a bar of chocolate from his
pocket. We sat down on the side of a snowy ditch and
divided it carefully into five even pieces. I felt as if my
life had been saved.

Finally my brother decided that it was time to go
home, a decision that I had come to about two hours
previously, but because I was only on a test run I had
kept my thoughts to myself. As we trudged homewards
I ached with tiredness and longed to just lie down and
go to sleep, but I followed the others and sometimes my
sister came back to give me a pull up a particularly
steep field. At last we saw the light of our own house
and I almost cried with relief; just a last spurt and we
would soon be there.

When we arrived in the door I could smell soup and I
had never before smelt anything as good. My mother
eased off the heavy, wet clothes; I had not realised what
a burden they had been until I was rid of them. Then
we sat around the table and she poured hot, thick soup
out of a big enamel jug into cups. There was eating and
drinking in it, and I told her that it was the most beautiful soup that I ever tasted. She smiled and said,
"Hunger is a great sauce." After the dinner we counted
the takings, and divided by five it was still a sizeable
amount, but even the thought of being rich was no sub-

stitute for sleep. All I wanted was to get into my bed and sleep. I had discovered that you needed long legs and stamina to go hunting the wren.

Days of Rest

O N THE FARM the days after Christmas were a
time of sleep and restoration for land, animals
and humans. Growth and productivity had
ceased, so we all hibernated. The fields and ditches retired under a blanket of snow. You walked out there
into a silent place and the only movement was the river
that wound like a black snake through the white farm.
All growth activity had retreated underground and the
only signs of life were the rabbit tracks in the snow and
sometimes larger ones to denote that a fox was in resi-

dence. No sound of bird life came from the icy branches, for they too seemed to have abandoned the outer spaces of the farm and had drawn in around the house, where they helped themselves from the pigs' troughs and picked up the scattered oats after the hens. Hens are early risers and normally in the morning when you opened the door of their house they were queued up waiting to pour out, screeching and cackling in delight; the snow, however, put an end to their early morning enthusiasm. When you threw open the door of their house on a snowy morning, instead of the tumbling flurry of white feathers as they jumped over each other in their hurry out, now they drew back in dismay, squawking disdainfully. They hated the snow and peered out in disgust and only a few of the braver ones ventured out; when their spindly yellow legs sank down into it they quickly returned to the security of their house. Once they were fed they flew back up on to their perches where they slept or gossiped among themselves. They refused to lay and decided that they were going to spend these days eating and sleeping until the world outside was back to normal.

The cows also adopted the hens' attitude, being fed in their stalls and only coming out once a day for water. The big job of the day was "tending the cows". Large pikefuls of hay were drawn across the haggard from the hay-barn to the stalls and then the channel that ran along behind the cows was brushed out and the big dunghill outside the stalls grew larger. The cows no longer yielded milk, so the main work of the farmyard, the morning and evening milking, was no longer necessary. Below the cow-house the horses, too, remained in the stables and came out only for water; the hay was thrown in through the window above their mangers and they crunched with satisfaction as they stood on three legs and rested the fourth, in rotation.

The land and the animals rested and we rested with them. Once St Stephen's Day had passed with its need for rising early to go hunting the wren, we slept late every morning and breakfast was usually at midday. The table was pulled up beside the fire so that we could make toast without having to move. It was a long and leisurely breakfast with books propped up against jugs, but the books were abandoned if Denis Brennan came on the radio to read a short story; his wonderful voice brought any story alive. Sometimes while we were still eating, Bill or some other neighbour called and the breakfast was further extended.

During the rest of the year, roving was normally done at night, but the days after Christmas were an exception to that rule. Now visitors came in the evening as the daylight waned and went home later when the

moon had risen to light their way. We were all on our
annual holidays, so we visited back and forth at odd
hours. Town cousins came on their Christmas visit and
we had a special tea in the parlour and stayed up late
to entertain them. On those nights we had lemonade
and biscuits after the tea and the adults had something
stronger. Everybody had to sing to provide entertainment, which was a bit tough on the crows amongst us
and harder still on the listeners. But the best night's
entertainment was when the big wrenboy group came
for a house dance. They packed the kitchen and filled it
with music and song and bounced off the stone floor in
complicated sets.

In the nights after that dance Bill tried to teach us
how to dance the sets to the music of a gramophone
record. The gramophone remained in the kitchen for
the duration of Christmas and we played it every night,
replacing the worn brass needles with new ones from a
small tin box with "His Master's Voice" printed on the
cover and the picture of a dog looking into a large horn.
The new needles we had got for Christmas were stored
in the gramophone beside the horn, which was lifted
back and forth when the record was changed. Sometimes if my father had to go to town for the New Year
he brought more new records, and one of these records
had a song which began

Shake the holy water, close the door:

The banshee is around tonight.

I didn't like this record at all because it scared me.
Often around the fire at night the neighbours told ghost
stories, and afterwards we would be so frightened going
up the dark stairs with the candle that we imagined we
saw all sorts of spooks watching us out of dark corners.
On those nights we checked behind the door and under
the bed for undesirable visitors. The man who spe-

cialised in ghost stories was Con, who lived across the river, and we loved it when he came, though it took us a few nights to recover from his visit. As we sat around the fire listening to his stories, I liked to sit beside my mother so that I could rest my head on her lap and she would run her fingers through my hair and massage my scalp. The soothing, comforting feeling made the ghost stories less frightening. Many of the emigrants home for Christmas came visiting and fascinated us with stories of London, New York and other far-away places.

On New Year's Eve my mother placed another large candle in the window to welcome in the New Year. The Christmas candle was now well burnt down as she had lit it every night. This new candle signalled a new beginning and we felt that we were putting the old year behind us and were going to put our best foot forward for the New Year. Now instead of wishing each other Happy Christmas, the neighbours wished each other Happy New Year, which I regretted as I did not like the idea of Christmas being replaced. But on New Year's Day, as on Christmas Day, we had a roast goose for the dinner and afterwards, as we had done every day since the snow had come, we fed the birds. We went out into the garden and scattered breadcrumbs on the snow under trees and then stood inside the kitchen window and watched them gather. Sometimes the crows swooped down and gobbled everything up in seconds so we had to maintain a supervisory eye on the feeding to guarantee fair play for the small ones. It was my dream to have a pet bird and I tried to capture one. Over the breadcrumbs outside the window I placed a box propped up by a stick and I tied a piece of string to the stick. I trailed the string across the garden path and in the kitchen window. The plan was that when a bird was under the box I would pull the string and the box would fall down and trap the bird. That was the theory but the practice resulted in broken sticks and cracked bits of string and airborne birds, so I came to the conclusion that I was not in the big game hunting league.

At night we sat around the fire reading books or playing cards. We played "forty-five", "donkey", "beggar-my-neighbour" and "a hundred and ten". We played under Bill's directions but did not take the games very seriously; as Bill himself took cards seriously, this annoyed him, and sometimes he banged down the cards and walked out on us. When this happened Dan used to say, "He's a bigger child than any of them." But Dan refused to play with us at all as he maintained that he would not be responsible for what he might do to us when we made mistakes. Bill was always back the night after, ready for another session. Snakes-and-ladders and ludo did not cause such friction and often we spent hours joining the dots in books of puzzles we had got from Santa, which Dan declared was the pastime of simpletons.

The last step of our Christmas journey came with Little Christmas and on Little Christmas Eve we lit our third and final candle in the window to replace the New Year candle. This was also Women's Christmas, and Dan declared that it was typical of the women to have their celebrations on the last day as they had to have the last word on everything. We believed that this was the night that Our Lord had turned the water into wine, so later that night we checked the bucket of spring water that had been brought earlier from the well to see if it had been changed into wine; despite great expectations the miracle of Cana was never repeated in our kitchen. Mrs Casey for her part believed that the souls of the dead were close to us on that night, and though we were not quite convinced, we were still slow to go out into the darkness on our own.

The following day we had our last Christmas dinner in the fading magic of a departing Christmas. That was the final night on which a candle would light in our window: it had glowed for the twelve days of Christmas, and tomorrow we would take down the decorations.

THE BOOKS OF ALICE TAYLOR

To School Through the Fields

"One of the most richly evocative and moving portraits of childhood [ever] written . . . A journey every reader will treasure and will want to read over and over again." *Boston Herald*

"A very special book by a very special author . . . Read between the anecdotes and you discover a complete philosophy for our time, with invaluable lessons on everything from childcare and parenthood to the importance of the natural environment and the infinite variety of human nature."
Writer's Monthly

ISBN 9780863220999

Quench the Lamp

"Taylor follows *To School Through the Fields* with these equally captivating further recollections of family life in pastoral County Cork, Ireland. Infused with wit and lyricism, the story centers on the 1950s when the author and her friends were budding teenagers. Taylor describes the past vividly and without complaint as years of hard labor for herself, parents and siblings, making clear that the days also were full of fun shared with neighbors in the close-knit community." *Publishers Weekly*

ISBN 9780863221125

The Village

"What makes the story unique is Taylor's disarming style; she writes as though she were sitting next to you, at dusk, recounting the events of her week . . . Taylor has a knack for finding the universal truth in daily details." *Los Angeles Times*

"She has a wicked wit and a pen which works on the reader slowly but insidiously." *The Observer*

ISBN 9780863221422

THE BOOKS OF ALICE TAYLOR

Country Days

"Like Cupid, the author has an unerring aim for the heartstrings; however, she can also transform the mundane into the magical." *The Irish Times*

"A rich patchwork of tales and reminiscences by the bestselling village postmistress from Co. Cork. Alice Taylor is a natural writer." *Daily Telegraph*

ISBN 9780863221682

A Country Miscellany

"Marries Richard Mills' breathtaking wildlife photos to the wellspring of Ms Taylor's stories from life." *RTE Guide*

"Excellently produced . . . this is a lovely book . . . an ideal present for the discerning reader. It is, in short, vintage Taylor." *Southern Star*

ISBN 9781902011080

The Parish

"Through a series of vignettes of life in her own village, Innishannon, Taylor explores the positive values of the social community that makes up the parish. Her story-telling ability lures us into a world of church fund-raising, Tidy Towns, local magazines, gardening and the myriad of activities at the heart of rural life." *Irish Independent*

ISBN 9780863223747

THE BOOKS OF ALICE TAYLOR

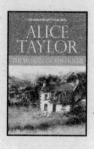

The Woman of the House

"An entrancing story written with much sensitivity and great depth of feeling, this is a delightful read." *Booklist*

"What shines through in *The Woman of the House* is Alice Taylor's love of the Irish countryside and village life of over 40 years ago, its changing seasons and colours, its rhythm and pace." *Irish Independent*

ISBN 9780863222498

Across the River

"Alice Taylor is an outstanding storyteller. Like a true seanchai, she uses detail to signal twists in the plot or trouble ahead. *Across the River* is the second volume in the saga of the farming Phelans and their neighbours . . . It is tightly plotted fiction, an old-fashioned page-turner with all the moral certainties of a fairy tale." *The Irish Times*

"A master of the genre." *Kirkus Reviews*

ISBN 9780863222856

House of Memories

"One of the strongest and most moving elements in *House of Memories* concerns the death of a much-loved character who featured in the two previous novels, and the grief experienced by those closest to him. It is an account that is both deeply felt and totally authentic."

"*House of Memories* shows her in her prime as a novelist." *Irish independent*

ISBN 9780863223525

PATRICK TAYLOR

An Irish Country Doctor

The *New York Times* bestselling novel that rivals
James Herriot

"At last! Here is an authentic Northern Ireland voice
telling down-to-earth stories that could have happened
anywhere on the island. A full cupboard of delightful
characters, both human and animal, enrich every page.
Quirky, funny, and deeply moving by turns, Taylor's writing perfectly
captures the language and characters of Ulster in times gone by."
Morgan Llywelyn

ISBN 9780863223938

BRYAN MACMAHON

Hero Town

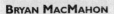

"For the course of a calendar year, Peter Mulrooney,
the musing pedagogue, saunters through the streets
and the people, looking at things and leaving them so.
They talk to him; he listens, and in his ears we hear the
authentic voice of local Ireland, all its tics and phrases
and catchcalls. Like Joyce, this wonderful, excellently
structured book comes alive when you read it aloud."
Frank Delaney, *Sunday Independent*

ISBN 9780863223426

JOHN B. KEANE

The Bodhrán Makers

The first and best novel from one of Ireland's best-
loved writers, a moving and telling portrayal of a rural
community in the '50s, a poverty-stricken people who
never lost their dignity.

"This powerful and poignant novel provides John B.
Keane with a passport to the highest levels of Irish
literature." *Irish Press*

ISBN 9780863223006

WALTER MACKEN

Rain on the Wind

"A raw, savage story full of passion and drama set amongst the Galway fishing community." *Irish Independent*

ISBN 9780863221859

The Bogman

"In *The Bogman* Macken explores the deep recesses of the land and people." Alice Taylor, *Irish Examiner*

ISBN 9780863221842

Sunset on Window-Panes

"In his company, to use a fine phrase of Yeats, brightness falls from the air." *Newcastle Chronicle*

ISBN 9780863222542